Daniel Miller

The Comfort of People

polity

Copyright © Daniel Miller 2017

The right of Daniel Miller to be identified as Author of this Work has been asserted in accordance with the UK Copyright, Designs and Patents Act 1988.

First published in 2017 by Polity Press

Polity Press
65 Bridge Street
Cambridge CB2 1UR, UK

Polity Press
101 Station Landing, Suite 300
Medford, MA 02155, USA

ISBN-13: 978-1-5095-2431-0
ISBN-13: 978-1-5095-2432-7(pb)

A catalogue record for this book is available from the British Library.

Typeset in 9.75 on 15pt Meridien by
Servis Filmsetting Ltd, Stockport, Cheshire
Printed and bound in Great Britain by Clay Ltd St. Ives PLC

The publisher has used its best endeavours to ensure that the URLs for external websites referred to in this book are correct and active at the time of going to press. However, the publisher has no responsibility for the websites and can make no guarantee that a site will remain live or that the content is or will remain appropriate.

Every effort has been made to trace all copyright holders, but if any have been inadvertently overlooked the publisher will be pleased to include any necessary credits in any subsequent reprint or edition.

For further information on Polity, visit our website:
politybooks.com

Contents

Acknowledgements

I am grateful to all the anonymous informants for this study, especially those terminal patients who agreed to give their precious time to these discussions. I am indebted to 'Maria', who jointly conducted with me all the hospice interviews and who commented on this manuscript. Also thanks to 'Dr Helena' who, much to my surprise, since I considered myself quite unsuited to the task, suggested that I should conduct research with hospice patients. Also thanks to the various nurses, here generalized as 'Justine'. I am also very grateful to Dr Ros Taylor MBE, Clinical Director of Hospice UK, who agreed to write a foreword to the volume.

I would like to thank Amelia Hassoun and Sabrina Miller who worked as interns, and especially Ciara Green, my co-researcher on the village ethnographic study who also undertook much of the transcribing of these interviews. I am grateful to those who have read the manuscript and made editorial comments: Amelia Hassoun, Rickie Burman, Laura Haapio-Kirk and Xinyuan Wang. The project forms one part of the Why We Post project and I am grateful for the support of the whole team and the funding from the European Research Council grant ERC-2011-AdG-295486 Socnet. Parts of the conclusion have been previously published as 'The Tragic Dénouement of English Sociality', *Cultural Anthropology* 30(2): 336–57.

Foreword

I have learnt over the years, as a hospice physician that, as life ebbs, connections become ever more important. Connections to family, friends, enemies and community. It's almost as if the energy to face loss is gathered from others.

These connections are hidden from health care, are often surprising and yet are such a valuable resource if only they are noticed. Doctors look at body parts, occasionally at the whole person, but almost never at the sustaining systems that surround people. Yet these systems can often be the clue to maintaining resilience or understanding distress in the face of advancing illness.

The Comfort of People reveals, in both technicolour and shades of grey, the ordinariness, the drama, the simplicity and the complexity of networks as people live out lives in the shadow of a serious diagnosis. These narratives of hospice patients, observed by an anthropologist, reveal the many ways in which people express themselves, choosing different media for different relationships: media such as Facebook to broadcast bulletins when close to death or Skype to connect with grandchildren around the world. The choice of communication channel seems to have meaning in terms of privacy, asymmetry, brevity and publicity. But ultimately these stories show that choices about communication and connection are pivotal to experiencing closure, and we should respect and understand the value and power of each – face to face, text, phone or Facebook.

Many of the findings were surprising to me: the reticence to invite people into their house, the 'Englishness' that Miller describes, contributes to a profound sense of isolation, even in a small village. People seem happier to connect in public spaces, or sometimes not at all. Miller observes that when the social relations of older people 'become attenuated, they cultivate their plants instead'. The garden seems a huge source of comfort and distraction.

The issue of 'confidentiality' is intriguing and highlighted in Marilyn's experience in story 3. Patients expect their vital medical information to be shared with all those who need to know – yet the 'cult' of confidentiality, as Professor Miller sees it, causes harm and frustration. It is quite remarkable that even as a patient is broadcasting details of her illness in a blog to the public, the doctor won't email her scan result to a neighbouring hospital. The 'devotion' to fax machines has to change!

These stories need to be read by all those working with dying people. 'It is only in the process of dying that she has resolved one of her main conundrums of living: how best to use time.' This insight from Miller jumped out at me.

We will be better healers if we realize the power, complexity and comfort of those in the patient's social universe. We are learning to ask 'What matters to you?'. These stories remind us to ask '*Who* matters to you?'.

Dr Ros Taylor MB, BChir, DL, MBE
Clinical Director, Hospice UK

Introduction

This is a book about people's lives, not their deaths. It is a book about hospice patients, rather than the hospice. The primary aim is to provide a sense of the social connections of individuals who are diagnosed with a terminal, or long-term, illness that has led them to become patients of a hospice. The book explores the comfort of people, but also the wider consequences of the presence or absence of others. A secondary theme is the impact of contemporary media because this book arose from an academic project, studying the use of media. Many of these social contacts are routinely maintained at a distance. Because I am an anthropologist and understand what I observe in terms of norms and expectations, this is thirdly a book about Englishness.

The why and the how

I had no intention of carrying out research with hospice patients. At the time, I was in receipt of an advanced European Research Council grant for a five-year study of the use and consequences of social media around the world (Why We Post). This included an 18-month study of people living in a village north of London.[1] It was during my fieldwork that I was approached by Dr Helena, the hospice director, to conduct research within the hospice and make some applied recommendations, which are found at the end of this volume.

What I had not appreciated, prior to this research, was how perfectly Dr Helena embodied the ethos and spirit of the hospice movement itself. I recall watching her talk at periodic hospice meetings for potential patients and their carers. These meeting are critical for reframing the hospice experience. After all, the hospice is defined as a place you become associated with when you have received a terminal diagnosis. Soon after we began research, I bumped into an elderly man who referred to the hospice as the 'knacker's yard,' which is an old English expression for the profession that turned dead horses into substances such as glue and fertilizer – hardly attractive connotations.

What Helena managed to do within minutes was to pirouette a 180-degree turn from downbeat to upbeat; she managed to make the hospice sound like fun. The core achievement of the hospice movement has been to shift people away from thinking about the period before death as the end of life and instead more as a new stage of life with its associated possibilities. If we imagine that it is a good thing to 'invest' in our children and their future, this might imply, by contrast, that once we know that someone is dying, they are no longer worth 'investing in'. Helena countered this by noting that once you have been diagnosed as terminal, you are actually entering an important stage

---

[1] The Why We Post project is being published in eleven volumes by UCL Press, including the comparative *How the World Changed Social Media* (Miller et al. 2016) and my own volume, *Social Media in an English Village* (Miller 2016). These are all available as free, open-access downloads from UCL Press.

in life, with all the possibilities that being alive brings: perhaps the time to have an exhibition of one's art, or marry the person you have grown increasingly fond of. This is a final opportunity to do something positive with life and we should seize it while we can.

The hospice had extensive medical back-up, such as specialist pain relief and physiotherapy, but was mainly there to give support and confidence back to its patients and their families. Not a place to die in so much as an institution that helped people to remain for as long as possible in their own homes – to live. As director of an English hospice, Helena also knew exactly how to transmit this idea and engage her audience. Her talk was very funny, using humour, banter and warmth to convey these messages. In many ways, the hospice is actually quite keen not to be overly associated with the word 'terminal'. Several of these informants had been patients for many years and some are likely to survive their cancer and return to a normal life and even a normal lifespan. The hospice is about promoting, not crushing, hope. It also deals with illnesses that people may not recover from but are gradual in their impact, representing sometimes decades of frailty that requires assistance.

Although the word 'hospice' was originally associated with Christian institutions for looking after the sick and dying, developed from medieval times, the modern hospice movement with which this book is concerned was founded by Dame Cicely Saunders (e.g. Saunders 2006) in the 1950s as a movement dedicated to people with terminal conditions. 2017 will celebrate the fiftieth anniversary of the establishment of the first purpose-built hospice in 1967. Subsequently, the modern hospice movement has become established in many countries around the world. Apart from being involved with medical research into issues such as pain control, the hospice movement advocated a move towards palliative care based on this more holistic ideal of end of life, something that would be much harder to achieve within the general hospital context. At least in Britain most people do prefer to stay in their own homes. Consequently, most hospice care consists of nurses going out to patient's homes, complemented by courses dealing with issues such as anxiety and physiotherapy, available at the hospice itself. Since so much of the work is based on outreach, the issue of communication is central to effective practice. This was the reason that Helena asked me to investigate the consequences of new media and its potential for the future of the hospice.

As it happens, I had felt frustrated for quite some time that my academic work had never had a directly applied outcome. My academic reputation was more as a theorist of material culture. I had managed to obtain grants for what could be regarded as strictly academic work, but all my previous attempts to raise money for carrying out more applied work had failed. Apparently, I am just not qualified to be useful, outside of education. But now I had funding for a five-year project and I figured no one would notice if I skived off and did a bit of applied work on the side. Working for the hospice became a kind of private vice that I wasn't really 'supposed' to have. Since this project was done in the interstices of my main fieldwork, it was quite stretched. The first interview took place in April 2012 and the last in December 2014. I had no intention of writing a book; the aim was to provide the hospice with practical advice which appears at the end of this volume.

It was obvious that, given my lack of experience with terminal patients, I should never interview a hospice patient on my own. We therefore agreed that all research would be carried out alongside a senior hospice professional, Maria, who had many responsibilities, ranging from bereavement counselling to organizing many of the courses that helped both patients and carers. Maria was extremely successful at her job, but was seeking an opportunity to carry out a more reflective, academic engagement to complement her other work. The interviews also gave her a chance to re-engage with some of her professional and academic training that had been neglected.

Maria was the perfect partner for this work. For one thing she has patience. She would spend ages going through consent forms, making very clear the nature of patients' involvement and that they could stop at any time, or retract their participation, and so on. I would have done this too but, to be honest, at about five times her speed. Alongside Helena, Maria showed me that just because someone is dying doesn't mean that the right tone is downbeat. Quite the contrary, patients are desperate to escape from being defined only by the fact that they are terminal and are often delighted to find that we had come to get their advice about something as future-orientated as new media. There were very few interviews that didn't include some jokes, sometimes quite rude ones, and laughter. Once I realized that, in almost every case, the patients seemed to have enjoyed themselves and were happy for us to return, I felt more confident that it was not inappropriate to engage in the informal and jokey upbeat style which, in any case, is probably the only way I know to carry out research. I don't really do downbeat.

As an experienced hospice professional, Maria was also expert at judging when the time was right to remind patients that perhaps they were feeling tired and would prefer us to return on another day. Maria also helped me get to know some of the hospice nurses and subsequently arranged for me to interview twenty of the staff, in this case without her being present. There were fifty patients involved in this research, most of whom had received terminal diagnoses and who have subsequently died, though some are now in remission. The dominant, but by no means the only, reason people were associated with the hospice was cancer.

Helena's brief was for us to investigate the potential of new media, which fitted with my larger ERC project. But as an anthropologist I assumed that you can only understand new media if you investigate people's relationships to all media. Furthermore, because this is all social communication, it makes no sense outside the context of people's wider social connections, including face to face. We didn't use any formal questionnaire, but the general pattern, for both Maria and myself, was at some time during our conversation to try and cover all the different ways people might communicate. Maria would also use her prior training in systemic family therapy to draft maps (genograms – see McGoldrick and Gerson 1985) of the entirety of an individual's social connections as these emerged from the interviews. Since this was intended as an applied project for the hospice, and not as an academic project, I did not initially publish any findings. Instead, I sent the report directly to interested hospice staff and posted it on my personal page of my department website (UCL Anthropology).

This book is clearly a kind of a praise poem to the hospice. I remain astonished that patients who knew they were dying and might have been expected to be resentful or angry never expressed anything but appreciation for the hospice itself, especially when one considers their initial reluctance to even be associated with the hospice, thereby explicitly acknowledging a terminal condition. Some patients, such as Chrissie (5), had still not been able to bring themselves to actually visit the hospice itself. It is to be hoped that this book's contents will also give readers some appreciation of the world of hospice nurses, here all referred to as 'Justine'.

The National Health Service (NHS) has a more ambivalent presence in this volume as, while the hospice often received praise, this was in contrast to the frustrations or problems associated with the wider health service. This volume includes one unequivocal critique which is that the NHS's obsessive concern with confidentiality is a cause of harm, which forms the substance of Marilyn's story (3).[2] In fact, most patients held the National Health Service in considerable esteem, and generally saw the defects either in terms of underfunding or of the de-humanizing that stems from huge-scale and necessary bureaucracy: for example, the lack of personal consideration given to former NHS staff, such as Veronica (2), when they have themselves become ill. It was salutary to compare my findings with those of an anthropologist working on dying in the United States. There, every story was dominated by issues of cost, which helped me appreciate that, thanks to the combination of a free hospice and free NHS, expense was almost entirely absent as a consideration in our interviews.

Ordinary death

One advantage of working through the hospice is that we had no say in the selection of patients other than a request that they should be from rural areas in order to match my wider research topic. Since everyone dies, there is nothing special about the

[2] Numbers refer to the chapters/stories.

people who appear in this volume. It is not just that they are ordinary people; this book focuses on the way in which dying itself is ordinary. Carrying out this research suggested that for most people dying is not an especially profound experience. I suspect we all have fantasies that if only we knew we were dying, then we would actually get round to having that special experience, devote ourselves to that welfare project, or write that piece which we always meant to do. But, generally, this is not what people subsequently do. If you want to do something special, then my advice is don't wait until you are diagnosed as terminal.

Even though we often talked about patients' lives as a whole, the tone was neither especially regretful, nor self-congratulatory, nor evaluative. Only two patients ever suggested that they had, or desired to have, some deeper conversations as a result of acknowledging that they were terminal. Most of the discussion was about everyday living. The substance was often pragmatic and the attitude usually phlegmatic. In any case, our choice of topic was more likely to lead to a conversation about social embarrassment, about people, including themselves, being unsure as to how one should behave in relation to friends and family, given these new circumstances, or conversation focused on trying to explain which relationships had been sustained and which had fallen away.

But could there be something profound about this evidence for ordinary death? The fact that people desire to maintain life, as it has been lived, does in and of itself represent a commitment. After all, why would, or why should, people repudiate what they are and have been, and how exactly would that help them at this point? By remaining true to what they have always been, people in some measure give value to their life as it has actually been lived. So this book attempts to pay respect to that which these patients understood themselves to be, mostly a modest engagement with life, which they simply wished to maintain while they still could. This is not a book for existentialists or others looking for meaning in death other than the very obvious lesson, which is to value life while we have it.

Englishness

There is a concluding section to this book which deals with a single finding that seemed to be the most surprising result of this research, requiring deeper examination. The conclusion investigates why some people with a terminal diagnosis find that, despite living in villages, they experience a degree of loneliness and isolation which seems to have arisen because of quite specific English sensibilities. This finding was not the result of any conscious plan or prior hypothesis. It just transpired that inadvertently we had hit upon the ideal way to study such a problem. I simply cannot imagine interviewing people with a terminal diagnosis directly about topics such as isolation and loneliness; it would be an extremely cruel confrontation. This book may give the impression that, because of the editing of these transcripts, we were confronting people with precisely this issue, but in fact we were careful not to do so. Instead, it was our method of systematically discussing each different medium in turn that allowed issues of loneliness to emerge without this becoming apparent. We were actually more concerned to keep the interviews relatively light and make sure people were comfortable and enjoyed the experience. Some people did, of their own volition, talk about feeling lonely and isolated, but that was simply because we presented an opportunity for them to discuss those feelings, which we certainly didn't want to foreclose.

The academic term for what we were studying is sociality. Our topic was the media, but these were always social media. Sociality is partly a description of people's social lives but, as a more abstract and academic term, it implies questions about why people do or do not socialize in particular ways. We need to also explain the patterns of socializing we uncover. So although every chapter appears to be a kind of vignette about an individual, these build towards a certain sense of typicality that needs to be accounted for, in some cases by asking questions about the nature of English sociality, in other cases considering the way new media have changed our social universe.

It is unlikely that we will understand the social relations of a person with a terminal condition simply by focusing on this particular stage in their lives. Mostly the reasons they have an extensive social network, or that their friendships derive mainly from their place of work, were already well established. Indeed, you will read more than one case where a patient argues that it was their parents or grandparents who set the pattern, for example regarding their particular concerns over respectability. Much of the content is also about individuals' self-characterization as self-sufficient and preferring their own company, or having a strong sense of either family or friendship. We shall see that it is a great mistake to assume that people who live in villages thereby live in communities. Some certainly do, but, as my other work shows, the proportion of contemporary villagers who are active in the communal side of village life is often surprisingly small. Despite the fact that people with a terminal diagnosis might be expected to develop or deepen religious sensibilities, there was very little mention made of religion.

Why does the conclusion focus specifically upon the nature of Englishness? Again this was inadvertent. For a period of eighteen months, I was carrying out research in a dual-village site I call The Glades for a book that has since been published called *Social Media in an English Village*. For much of this time, I spent one day a week working with these hospice patients and, in order to justify this, requested that where possible they come from villages similar to The Glades. All my previous ethnographic experience in England had been in London, and I had chosen The Glades for reasons of logistics. I had no idea that I would encounter a place where less than 2 per cent of the population were from ethnic minority backgrounds, as confirmed by local medical statistics. The hospice patients came from a similar population, relatively affluent, and almost entirely born in England. None of the people who appear in this book are migrants or descended from recent migrants, and none are black or Asian. I therefore decided to take advantage of this opportunity to research, amongst other things, the nature of this home-counties, regional, non-cosmopolitan 'Englishness', something that is now quite rare even amongst the English. This is the topic that forms the book's conclusion.

The media

If the end point of this research is an understanding of the social lives of patients, the means to this end was a study of the impact of the media that have become the primary ways people are in contact with each other. From the beginning, that included discussion of face-to-face contact. As an anthropologist, I cannot regard face-to-face communication as unmediated. It comes with a whole slew of cultural rules about what is and is not appropriate behaviour. As will become clear, it is often conversation via phone, webcam, or texting that is more intimate than conventional face-to-face encounters. So, in reading this book, think of 'face to face' as one more type of media, rather than merely an absence of media.

There is a huge amount of material in this book about how people use different media. The evidence shows clearly why it is not possible to simply separate out a thing called 'social relationships' as opposed to the media through which they are increasingly practised. The mere fact that some of the patients have such close relationships with friends and relatives in places as far away as Australia demonstrates the way inexpensive new media have reduced geographical obstacles to intimacy. Matt (18) used to tell me that during chemotherapy he simply couldn't sleep, and he really needed the company of people who were awake in the middle of the night on the other side of the planet, which was now easy to find. On the one hand, several elderly patients suggested that the one compensation for dying was that people would stop trying to force them to use new-fangled media such as computers, while, by contrast, Jeanette and Bernard (14) happily saw the potential of new media for purposes such as appreciating classical music.

The evidence also warns against conservatism. This book shows how it was actually the traditional telephone that was in some ways extremely un-English because it was exceptionally intrusive. With landlines, we don't know in advance when would be a convenient time to speak. It is much more English to be able to text or WhatsApp in advance to minimize intrusion. So there are many points that will emerge about the media. But this does not form the conclusion of this book simply because that was the task of the recently published *Social Media in an*

English Village. But it may be helpful in reading what follows to appreciate the perspective that I brought to the encounter, which is encompassed by the term 'polymedia'.

Polymedia is a word coined by Mirca Madianou and myself (Madianou and Miller 2012a, 2012b) as the conclusion to a research project we previously conducted with Filipina women living in England, who were parenting their left-behind children in the Philippines through new media. The book tells us as much about being a mother as about the media. I prefer not to invent words, but there was simply no other way to make our point. Most people will ask questions about each individual media platform, such as the landline or Facebook, and mainly about whether we think these are good or bad. But, reading these stories, one can see why such questions don't work. People have different ways of using each platform and different views as to their consequences. Instead, these stories suggest that we need a more holistic perspective. We can only understand people's relationship to something like WhatsApp when we set this against all the other media that these patients use, such as voice calls or webcam, and try and understand why they have email friends as opposed to phone friends.

Polymedia provides this holistic sense of multiple media which are typically employed in a complementary fashion. Elizabeth (13) uses Facebook to tell many people her news, while Celia (8) uses a group email for the same purpose. Polymedia is also used as a means for controlling relationships. An obvious example is Emma (10), who uses texting as the master medium for organizing all her relationships. Helen (15) makes the point that sometimes the aim of this control is simply to keep everyone at a distance when you need time and space to face things such as pain or depression on your own.

Such choices always have additional considerations, such as questions about using the 'right' media for the occasion, or worries about politeness and avoiding offence. The availability of polymedia means that we have an array of media choices; as a consequence, we will be judged as to which media we employ. This has become a moral issue in a manner that was not true when it was assumed people chose their media for reasons of cost or access. It is also possible to let certain media stand out as special, and for many elderly patients the time and effort of handwriting has become treasured, partly because it has also become rare. So, ultimately, polymedia allows us to approach media not in themselves but as an integral part of what makes social relationships possible, fraught, successful, intermittent, and often comforting.

There is no such thing as a pure social or human relationship – they are always mediated and material. Forget the media and return to the earlier discussion of Englishness. There are always issues of etiquette, rules about what can or cannot be said, spatial contexts such as being inside the house, or on the street, or in the hospice, that have a huge influence upon each conversation and relationship. To give just one example, none of this research would have been possible and much of the content would have been different without sensitivity to the role of humour. The first paragraph of this book confronts us with an example of particularly black humour from Sarah. In every interview, humour had a role in helping people to express and deal with their feelings regarding their illness. Humour is a medium.

Patients often made very clear that they also felt a relationship to the medium itself. We like or hate Facebook, feel self-conscious or at ease on the phone. Emma (10) certainly has a powerful relationship to her iPad, as did others, not included here, to their Kindle or to Radio 4. Of huge importance are people's feelings about their home and why they want to stay there, despite being ill. Another important relationship may be to their pet. We will encounter Bernard's (14) intense relationship to the repairing of clarinets, which is clearly enormously enriching. The conclusion reached by my previous book, *The Comfort of Things* (Miller 2008), was that people gain most from a few deep and sustained relationships, which can indeed be to things, or homes, or pets, or media and not just to other people. By contrast, dispersed shallower sets of relationships seem less fulfilling in the longer term, whether these are with people or things. What I did not find in previous research or in the work described here is that people's relationship to things, or to the media, was at the expense of the depth of their relationships to other people, something that is otherwise commonly assumed to be the case.

How I wrote this book

Even though much of the content of this volume is presented as interview transcripts within quotation marks, not every word is as it was spoken. There are several grounds for editing the interviews. Speech is often messy and unclear and I have freely added or left words out where I feel this clarifies the evidently intended meaning of what was said. I have not used ellipsis to indicate the many sections that have been edited out. I have reordered and collated sections, for example when a person spoke about the same topic at different stages of an interview. I have not included questions that we asked. Instead, I have sometimes added a few words to make clear what the patient was referring back to in their discussion.

The main changes that have been made to the text are, however, the results of a different concern, which is to ensure the anonymity promised to all informants, apart from in the final story of Matt. When something is pertinent to the topic of the discussion, I have tried not to change it, but otherwise many details have been altered in the interests of disguising the speaker. If the fact that a person was a management consultant seemed highly relevant, then I have felt it important to keep that information unchanged. But if they just happen to have been a baker without any wider implications, I may well have changed them into a butcher. Many other details will have been changed, such as the gender of a relative, or their place of origin. The intention is that no one should be able to recognize an individual from the account given here. The book is not, however, a work of fiction since everything it contains is designed to convey that which was actually observed or said.

For the same reason, although the stories appear to represent distinct individuals, in many cases they include material from different patients. Again, I have tried to think whether the result distorts the implications of that content. But quite often when people are talking about something specific, such as the use of a webcam or the effect of working in the community, it seemed reasonable to combine interesting observations from two different people. All names of persons and places are changed. Helena, Justine and Maria are also pseudonyms.

My attitude to ethics is very simple. I certainly make sure I am aware of formal ethical guidelines but, ultimately, I follow a single consistent rule, which is that one's research should never result in harm to people. Every ethnographic study is different, and the anthropologist should work hard to be sensitive to the sensibilities of their informants, rather than sticking to preor-

dained ethical rules. I have especially concentrated on anonymity where there is content that might be disparaging, or
in some other way cause hurt or harm. In such cases, if this
required drastic changes, such as altering the gender of the
person concerned, then I would have done that. But most of the
content is innocuous and I do not see it representing a potential
cause of harm. Rather, I hope it will have value for the purpose of education and practical improvements to hospice care,
as was indicated to our informants as the aim of our research.
This means one should be cautious in altering such stories.
For example, censoring negative content alone would obviously
lead to an overall misrepresentation of the lives of people with
terminal diagnoses, which would diminish the book's educational potential. One of the more surprising lessons from this
book, summarized in the third story, is that an over-concern for
confidentiality has itself become one of the primary causes of
harm to patients.

Story 1

Sarah

It was six days before her death. We didn't know it would only be six days, but we knew that Sarah would not grace us with her presence for much longer. And yet the temptation is to describe the occasion as rather lovely and certainly fun. She had offered us each a glass of Prosecco, and had a small one herself, perfect for a pleasant ambience, sitting in the back garden of her village home on a warm summer's day. But the real setting was this combination of Irish openness in speaking about death and an English love of black humour. She is talking about what will happen to her corpse: 'No reason why you can't put me in the dining room. I'll be very quiet. I'll be good. . . . He's going to put me in a pair of pink silk pyjamas. I have never worn a pair of pink silk pyjamas in my entire life. Not too worried what shade it is.' She tells of a recent expedition to the pub, where the family all went by car, leaving 'one skinny terminal' to jog her way up the hill. Listening now to those two hours of recorded conversation, the dominant sound is of constant banter and laughter, Sarah reporting the look on the face of that girl at the funeral parlour when she realized that the funeral Sarah was organizing was for herself. Black humour gets us through life – and death.

Still, as with all humour, the timing has to be right, and the place. One of the leitmotifs of this conversation is Sarah getting things wrong. As she remarks, it is partly because when you are terminally ill for such a long time, you tend to live within a bubble of people who are always appraised of this situation. So you may forget that others are ill prepared. One place where she got it wrong was the pub. Someone asked her how she was. The trouble came when she actually bothered to answer in some detail. One of the women there started to shake and tell her to 'stop it, stop it', that she 'can't take this', that 'it's too close to what happened to her mother'. Everyone was in tears. Clearly, there are limits and rules to pub banter; flirting and football are fine, but apparently not death, not even as jokes.

Sometimes it's the other way around. People expect to visit you in a hospital; it seems the right time to do this, without invading the privacy of the home. We know the drill, even if we forget that these days flowers are no longer allowed, which is really annoying. But the hospice is different. Terminal care is almost entirely in one's own home; people tend to come to the hospice only for brief periods to control pain, or regain some energy or take up various kinds of outpatient and activity sessions, such as counselling. So, unless this is literally the death-bed scene, it is actually a time when you probably don't want to see anyone at all. But when Sarah last went in, she had nine visitors on the first day. Fortunately, after that her ever-loving and highly sensitive husband put a stop to it. She had made a rather crucial mistake. She had posted on Facebook that she was going into the hospice so everyone immediately knew and this had caused the crush.

In every other respect, Facebook was a gift, a gift to Sarah and from Sarah, but then giving is what Sarah is all about. She was diagnosed with cancer ten months previously, and this was confirmed as terminal four months before we met. It's clear in retrospect that much of her time has been spent trying to think of ways that this terminal prognosis could be turned into something of value to others. But she would never in a million years have predicted that the means to achieve this would be Facebook. In fact, up to that moment she had never been on Facebook. It was the perspicacity of her son who had set up a Facebook account on the day of her diagnosis. Quite quickly, she sensed how this new relationship with people outside could transform her relationship to what was happening to her inside. Facebook would be her extended voice teaching the world about something that they needed to hear and were reluctant to confront, which was the experience of cancer and dying. Sarah was as aware as anyone about the need for this, having spent more than thirty years as a nurse and having witnessed the ignorance, misconceptions and denials. So Facebook would give her a final purpose, a means to turn all this negativity into something positive.

Despite their protestations to the contrary, it often tends to be older women who take as ducks to Facebook's water. This is *social* media, and in most families it's the women who do the business when it comes to keeping the conversations going, the business of simply being social. It's one of the comments the family often made about Sarah, well before Facebook. She was the glue, the chain, the one who kept the extended and extensive family linked, beyond the weddings and the wakes. She knew what had happened to whom and she told the others; not gossip, just the kind of sharing that makes family something more present and real. When trouble had come to one part of the family, she had been the person who had helped those children get through their parent's divorce. So a new technology that could bring with it a network of people and enable them to feel closer just fell straight into her lap. Her son knew that the best gift was to help her with the technology in setting up this new Facebook account, while her daughter is the one who helps her use it to maintain the social connections over the long term.

The story is there, scrolling through her Facebook account. It starts with a gradual build-up of people, though there were newcomers joining right up to her death. Lots of positive messages respond to the postings about her scans and chemotherapy:

'Sarah, what a joy to see your beautiful smile. All the Ryans on this side of the pond are holding every positive thought for you and sending them with wings of love.'

'Sarah, you are a healer and have been there for many people, including me! Your strength is admired and your spirit is strong . . . It is time for the universe to deliver some good karma for you.'

There was plenty of hope in that initial period. On the one hand, Facebook became an effective way to keep people appraised without having to tell them individually. Being a nurse, Sarah had no qualms about including the details.

Good news is 'no cancer spread', just isolated to the lower half of my stomach. The chemotherapy should help to reduce the thickness of my stomach lining and prevent further tumour cells or spread. They will check my response to treatment with a CT scan following 4 cycles of chemo and blood tests through monitoring tumour markers . . . I have completed the first of the three chemos via a drip over 15 mins, then the second over 2 hours, all seemed to be going well, then I experienced broncho spasm (couldn't breathe or swallow). TERRIFYING. The nurses and doctors responded quickly with oxygen, injections of hydrocortizone and Piriton, also warm blankets.

But this is constantly interlaced with humour: 'Tried on wigs at Selfridges post scan today, I looked a right Herbert – think I'll go bald in next three weeks with as much dignity as I can muster; depends on the shape of my head.' Sarah was as good as her word; she went for the bald look. It wasn't that this appealed to her in any way, she just felt wigs were still worse.

As requested, others respond with their jokes:

Knock, knock
Who's there?
Eileen
Eileen who?
Eileen on the bar while you buy the drinks

The close relationship with her husband and children is touching. Sometimes it isn't even clear if it is Sarah or her husband who is posting the news. They clearly share everything, including the Facebook account and password. You can also feel how all members of this group, through their responses, are doing all they can, just willing their words to turn things around for Sarah. There is so much wanting to do something, to say something. 'You are the most inspiring person I have met ever in my life. Now is the time, Sarah, for everyone to bounce back to you every ounce of love and healing right your way!!! So brace yourself girl, I am sending it to you by special courier; her name is faith. xxxx'

But, while the words help, they cannot heal, and the news gets worse until:

> I have been discharged by the surgeons and referred to the oncologists for palliative chemo, but have already decided to refuse. I want to claim my body back now and go with it. Sorry since the 9th Jan, my surgery, if I have acted out, but I am still in shock and hugely upset with the inoperable result. It's a shock. If you were in my boots, how would you feel? Anyhow looking for a hotspot in Europe to go and relax and enjoy what's left. xxx

Even with this, one of the worst communications anyone could receive, there is always the sense that the pill must be sugared with humour in order to be swallowed. 'Had holy communion but unfortunately my mobile phone went off with some rock song.' 'Thanks, Jean, for the laughter this morning; you can be absolutely hilarious and such great fun. Better medicine than any hospital has ever given me. Keep it up, I need it.'

Against her doctor's advice, she and her husband settle for a last Mediterranean holiday, and a mass of photos are posted of them by the pool and clearly enjoying the break. This itself was something of a final triumph since, days before she went, her doctors had been insisting that all food and drink would from now on only be ingested through a tube and she had insisted on taking the tube out. But it was also a triumph with respect to Facebook as it was only thanks to this holiday that she had finally been able to participate in 'normal' Facebook, posting those very ordinary shots of cocktails and swimsuits that everyone else gets to post. Just for a couple of weeks, her Facebook looks like Facebook is supposed to look. But then there is the inevitable return. We had not expected to see ourselves incorporated into the very stuff that we were studying, even prior to our first meeting. Clearly, Sarah had carefully read our introductory materials.

> Meeting with the research team today. I have already been advised that it can be exhausting, or may be emotional answering questions, and I can pull out at any time if it gets too much. Me thinketh they have no idea what they are letting themselves in for. I am not the one that will be emotionally drained or exhausted, so bring it on.

What you experience on Facebook is her honesty about the steps and stages that have to be accepted, dragging you to a place you haven't the slightest desire to reach but which keeps getting closer. A time comes when drinking a glass of champagne makes her vomit, at which point she posts that dying really is a 'pain in the arse'. Of course, it gets still worse:

> I am feeling quite ill and weak now, not myself, quite emotional. The drug they have me on is like speed, so can really affect your emotions and make you feel very tired. Last night I was quite symptomatic with sickness, reflux and diarrhoea, so I am not on form. I would like to send my husband, children and grandchildren a big hug to let them know how much they mean to me. xxxxx

The appeal of Facebook lies in her insistence that dying is something to be open about. Having previously worked in the health service, she has the experience and feels it has given her strength. For her, the crucial point is that most people don't have to confront these things and, without comparative experience, they are even more scared and anxious. She is sure there is a benefit to sharing her death and also her acceptance. She tells us how important this is with respect to her own family's response. 'I don't care if I am incontinent, or burping or letting out nasty noises; it's part of death. I have looked after people to the very end and given them the best death that they can possibly have and all I am asking for is a good death, a sweet ending, where my family aren't going to suffer too much.' She feels there is an additional suffering that comes from denial and avoidance and is lessened by acknowledgement and presence. Facebook gives her that presence, makes her gradual demise visible and so also meaningful.

The hospice becomes increasingly important. Earlier on she had noted, 'A big day yesterday; met with the hospice team re my future care and management. They already understand that I want to live my life fully and will only call them when I need them. Hopefully that is a long way off yet.' When that time comes she posts: 'Good news. I am getting oral fluid down and hope to go home tomorrow, God willing. Mind you, have met some lovely fellow patients and nurses, had a right laugh.'

> What a beautiful sunny day. I've stopped taking some of the medication (steroids) that has been causing me mood disturbances, tearfulness and fatigue; also stopping the antibiotic because it is making me sick. These things may alleviate some symptoms but they create more havoc with others. It's about knowing your body and its likes and dislikes. There is no use prolonging your life if it deteriorates the quality of it. Enjoy the sunshine today, it's a new day.

Finally, you know it is her husband who is posting: 'I'm hugely saddened in having to let everybody know that Sarah passed away at approximately 4.20 a.m. today. The family would like to thank everybody for the messages of support, thoughts & prayers that have given us so much strength. It has really meant so much to us all, but especially Sarah.'

The next few days sees a flood of posts. Even the most sceptical can see the potential of Facebook as a site where people who live too far away, or who cannot come to the funeral for other reasons, can at least express something of what they feel. 'Sorry I wasn't able to make it along yesterday to pay my respects personally but Sarah was in my thoughts and prayers throughout the day. God speed her wherever she heads next.' Many images of candles follow, but also glasses of champagne. Later on, there is fundraising for the hospice, and acknowledgement of the birthday that Sarah didn't live to see, 'Thinking of you, Auntie Sarah. Sending love and positive thoughts out into the universe in honour of your birthday and burning a flame in honour of you tonight.' Then more memories, more acknowledgements and, in the end, just the desire to retain something of the good that was Sarah.

Reading her posts and the responses, it becomes clear why for Sarah Facebook was nothing trivial, but as with the hospice itself, she felt that the period of her dying had enabled her to discover new things that were both profound and good. She tells us, 'For me, what I write on Facebook comes from my inner thoughts, more like reading a book. Created in my head, it's my feelings and thoughts at their purest. I may not have something to say every day . . . It's through Facebook that a lot of these people have rolled back into our lives. It's incredible.' What Sarah and her husband realized is that over the years they had developed many good close friendships. But there had been a natural attrition as people moved or kids grew up. But in many cases the closeness remained, and some of those who were most effective in using Facebook to give support and show how much they cared were people they hadn't actually been much in touch with recently. So instead of friendship representing the transience of their current network, it was like all the best people from all those different pasts coming together to remind them of the whole 54 years that were now coming to an end but which had been so full, not least of people and love. Facebook's resumé of life seemed to keep the best friends and allow those who should be forgotten to be forgotten. Reversing Shakespeare's Mark Antony, it is the good that we do that lives on, while the bad can be interred with the bones.

Sarah also came to appreciate that Facebook is not just one thing. She notes that different people have responded to particular elements that they feel they can connect to. One of her friends joined her on Facebook but clearly didn't really know what do with this medium, at least until Sarah started posting photos of the beautiful gardens that surround the hospice, which really are quite special. Then he too started taking photos of nature and found this was the medium where he could contribute. Another friend who had tended towards depression started to send Sarah messages on Facebook of a kind that she would never have imagined possible from him. Somehow following her process of dying had allowed him to rise back up to the surface of life. She also appreciated the potential of a digital legacy. At one point, she notes, 'When I die, it will go on Facebook.'

She appreciates the practical side too. When you are terminal you become so beholden to others, so if there is any way she can in turn support her husband or family, then that seems like an unalloyed blessing. Very soon she realizes that Facebook helped them as well as her:

> As soon as I got diagnosed, we're just being inundated with phone calls. So you can imagine how exhausting it is saying the same story over and over and over again. You're trying to come to terms with your own feeling and your own sense of loss and what's going on. And you're having to repeat it to family and friends, and we come from a large family and have a lot of friends. And they mean well, every one of them, but you are repeating that story over and over again. He [Sarah's husband] was getting it, my daughter was getting it, text message, phone calls. And they were being bombarded.

So the ability to give this level of detail and sheer reportage on one place at one time also acts as a gift to those who are having to spend so much time supporting her and acting as her voice to the world.

Most important of all is that Facebook sets into reverse the normal trajectory of dying. As Sarah had seen again and again:

> So I was saying that when you become ill you go through all these losses, like loss of job, company car, and your earnings. And your network of people that you're with every single day. Everything you do, used to go through, the country lanes, to my job. I just loved my life. I really loved my life. And suddenly bit by bit these things are taken away. That's the start of it and then, when it comes to your health, it's your energy levels and your symptoms of how you're feeling, not being able to eat. It's difficult going to restaurants like we've always done – that was our pleasure. You

know, the fatigue, not being able to do what we used to do. So it can isolate you. We try to be careful about what I do and what I don't do. My family have been very good with me. It has been a bunch of losses.

Usually, it is one's own network that starts to diminish because one becomes more immobile and cannot go out and socialize or visit people. But, with Facebook, the opposite seems to happen just when it is needed. 'And what this has done is bring us all together and connected us, particularly the nieces and the nephews. My sisters and brothers are all much older than I am. So [for them] this type of mode of communication is not very good. But their children communicate through this with me. And it's amazing.' It goes beyond that. Like any family there have been rifts, people who have stopped speaking to each other for many years. Who won't now even acknowledge each other. But such quarrels are put in a different perspective when people come together again to support someone who is dying. Sarah knows that this Facebook site will leave a legacy of repair and renewal with regard to her more extended family; she has already seen this with respect to several relationships. People who had not communicated for years had come to share this common Facebook space and sometimes, due to her own admonishments, had publicly become reconciled under her tutelage. Being able to effect these repairs to the family through the impact of her own dying made her very happy indeed.

Sarah is very much aligned with the ethos of the hospice itself that dying is a stage of living. But is it going to be a stage that shrinks people down till they fade from sight? Or a final chance to expand oneself and the world? In precise accord with the hospice director, Sarah's clear desire is to use Facebook to make more of life while she still can. It forms one part of her general attitude to this acknowledgement of dying itself as something which, like any stage of life, can either be lived to the fullest or wasted.

He says to me, 'You have advanced cancer! Take some drugs!' And I'd take paracetamol. The reason being is I want to be here! They've taken everything else, this disease has taken everything. It's not going to take that. Why would I take stuff that makes me sleep? Why do I want spend what is left of my life snoring my head off up there? When I can be down here having fun with you lot? It shows people that you may have been given a diagnosis and a prognosis but you're still here, still in that body, still with your ideas and points of view, and you're still living.

Even amongst the reticent English, the Facebook page of someone dying gives us licence, courage to become fulsome, to praise and to be emotional. As Sarah says many times, Facebook can allow things to be said that are simply not spoken face to face. Towards the end, she reads an example out in full from one of the comments on the site:

I also want to let you know how much I admire you. I'm so amazed at how you have galvanized friends and family and provided them with the platform to communicate and show support. So often in situations like this, people don't know how to be involved or whether to get in touch as they are not sure what to say. Yet you have encouraged people to interact and been very open and honest. I cannot imagine what you, your husband and children are going through. However, I'm in awe of the way that you have shared your feelings. I really hope that from this other people, who often feel alone or isolated when going through something as devastating as what you are, will be inspired to use social networking to do something similar.

As Sarah notes, 'I think she just said it all.'

Story 2

Champneys for the Terminal

The introduction to this book makes clear that my subject is hospice patients, not the hospice itself. But it would be churlish to not also acknowledge patients' feelings towards the hospice, which were overwhelmingly positive. Veronica, in her fifties, was a nurse with the National Health Service.

Veronica remarked about the hospice being a 'Champneys for the terminal' (Champneys is the name of a luxury spa resort). This was just one variation of something that I heard on many occasions. More commonly, patients said the hospice was a really pleasant place to stay, like a fine hotel, where the only drawback was that you had to be terminally or very seriously ill in order to stay there. The hospice certainly looks the part. It has an army of volunteer gardeners, and the grounds are exquisite with ponds and flower beds. If there is one thing English volunteers do exceptionally well, it is gardening. The hospice frontage does look rather like a hotel and the rooms have individual names.

Some of this is good fortune. It seems as though the hospice movement has inadvertently come up with the world's best business plan. This all starts with the hospice giving really good care and support to people who have advanced cancer or a terminal diagnosis. Then, after the patient dies, the relatives often feel an immediate sense of gratitude and debt, and at that point have a strong desire to repay this with donations, which may coincide with being the beneficiaries of some sort of inheritance from the deceased. This continual flow of money allows the hospice to employ more and better staff and additional support systems or ancillary services such as specialist pain control or counselling services. In turn, this leads to still better treatment and consideration for their patients, which then makes the new patients and their families even more concerned to repay this debt with still more substantial donations. This virtuous circle becomes almost a spiral when the setting is one of the most affluent areas of England. As a result, the hospice can employ 120 staff, largely funded by voluntary donations. I recall talking to an oncologist who was clearly a little resentful that there has been a shift in funding from cancer research to the hospice sector. Just occasionally, the good fortune leaks away in another direction, when patients make the mistaken presumption that the nursing care they have received from the hospice staff was provided by Macmillan, mainly because Macmillan have a still higher profile in advertising themselves as a charity than does the hospice.

This is hugely important from the perspective of patients. I was once at a conference comparing notes with a US anthropologist who was studying hospices. He found that one of the most common topics of conversation was money and the problems that people have in being able to afford their care. A novel by Lionel Shriver, called *So Much for That*, eloquently describes the oppressive presence of cost and debt as now integral to the experience of dying in the United States. It has become all about money. It was only during that conversation that it struck me that, in the two years of my own research, there had been barely any mention of money or cost. Between the National Health Service and the hospice movement, it was taken for granted that everything is free. So this may be an inadvertently brilliant business plan but the main result is that no patients have to confront this period of their lives from the perspective of a business. It is not even as though the hospice makes all the claims it could. Despite working with them, I had no idea until recently that the hospices were also involved in improving palliative care within the hospital sector.

Helena, the hospice director, took none of this for granted. At the time we were working together, she was also making trips advising the nascent hospice sector in one of the poorest areas of India. Here she was exposed to the other extreme, where the most fundamental requirement of a dying person, that is the provision of effective opiates for pain relief, are often absent because the hospices can't afford or can't obtain supplies. So even in this day and age, many people throughout the world die in an agony that could easily be avoided just by ensuring a global supply of opiates.[3] This is why the UK hospice movement works to spread the benefits of some of its own relative affluence to areas of deprivation. At the same time, hospices within the United Kingdom still only cover around a third of deaths and would be very willing to substantially increase that proportion and advance support to some of the more difficult areas, such as dementia care.

Yet, as an anthropologist, I felt that the single most interesting

[3] *The Economist* recently discussed this appalling situation: http://www. economist.com/news/international/21699363-americans-are-increasingly-addicted-opioids-meanwhile-people-poor-countries-die

thing about the hospice movement was that its key contribution had nothing at all to do with money. It hadn't cost a penny. The hospice really came into being simply through a reconceptualization of being terminal as a period of life. The point of the hospice movement is to address the medical issues as a necessity, but also as the background to their primary concern, which is to advance a more holistic and humanistic sense of well-being. The main task is one of reconceptualization of this as a period of life in terms of its opportunities for living, not dying. As an academic, I am fascinated by what has been achieved through changes in the perspective rather than through resources. The National Health Service is vast in scale, and the requirements of professional management can sometimes lead to a dehumanization of its work, which is exposed in areas such as palliative care. When Veronica compares the hospice to Champneys, it is not in fact the luxury side of things she wants to convey. It is the commitment to an ideal of well-being.

Veronica was in a good place to make the comparison since she had spent her entire working career as a nurse within the National Health Service. As a result, while others showed some reluctance to approach the hospice because doing so was intimately associated with an acknowledgement of their terminal diagnosis, she immediately sought it out.

I made the contact with the hospice last July when I was diagnosed, almost immediately after. I wanted the nurse to see me as I was before I became really unwell, before I started my treatment. Which I think Justine has found quite interesting. She has seen me right from the beginning, before anything started. Every week we've had contact. During my chemotherapy was the worst period. Through that, she came nearly every week, certainly if I needed her. If she wasn't visiting, I would talk to her by phone. Reasonably long chats, as long as I needed. More often than not she'd say, 'I'm coming round to see you' because she's very caring and, you know, I only really rang Justine when I didn't feel very well. So she felt she needed to come round. We exchanged mobile phone numbers when I first met her. Well, I know the hospice anyway. I've had a couple of friends who have died there. I have patients sent there. I did a charity thing there a year ago with a friend of mine. The town is very supportive of the hospice. It's a big thing. I'm going for the Alexandra technique, alternative therapies. With cancer, when you have chemo, you are offered a lot of nice things: alternative therapies, physio and acupuncture.

I've met so many people in different departments I've been visiting. Patients who have not had help like I've had. And I say, 'You've got to contact a Macmillan nurse, you've got to have one. Go and do it.' I met this woman at the clinic who was in pain. She'd told me she'd had breast cancer. She had told me about the pain in her legs. She said, 'My consultant just told me to put up with it; it'll go eventually.' I said, 'You're joking. Please, please, go see a Macmillan nurse. You've got to.'

I think this HOPE course will help me make friends. I smoke and Justine wants me to stop. She rang me today. So, yes, I think there is a chance there will be friendships from the hospice through the course. I think you get a real funny low when you recover because suddenly everything stops. Like an anti-climax. I've been extremely spoilt during my illness and made to feel very special. There's eight of us, and the ladies who run it. They have things they are going to go through, but it fires off with us. It's lovely, actually. The day I went to my last radiotherapy, I can't really describe it, but I was very emotional when I walked out. Felt like I was leaving a very special place behind. I was going for 10 months.

And everybody had been lovely there, and I actually felt very emotional.

•

Veronica is concerned about the possibility of being able to go back into her professional capacity. It seems that much of her anxiety comes from the contrast between her experience of the hospice as against her relationship with her own employers within the National Health Service.

But work has let me down big time. Very big time. And they are going to know about it. I haven't heard from my manager since September, and I've worked 22 years. So that really is something that's hurt me a great deal. Though [her manager] was very interested in the beginning to find out the gossip, if you like, 'Oh, what's happening?' And I gave her all the information. And then she just wasn't interested any more. She was my ward manager at one point. We always exchanged Christmas cards. Went out socially with a group of people. She wasn't a best friend, she was a colleague, but I did consider her a bit more than that. Forget that she's a friend or not a friend, somebody I know well. I think there has been nothing to make sure I'm OK, nothing since September. I think a letter wouldn't have hurt, really. The managers are managers and they are meant to look after their staff. I did get a card from work eventually. And some flowers. That took quite a long time. The matron, who's my senior manager, hasn't bothered. The ward manager, in fairness to her, I only met her six weeks before I went off sick.

I don't have a lot of close friendships with people I work with, but I do have several. And those have been in touch with me. I was talking about that again today actually because when people go off and have a baby, and you think, oh my goodness, they are coming back to work and the baby is six months now and I haven't rung them – but they're not close friends. So I can understand when it is people who are not close friends. I've had texts and emails from colleagues, yes. But my manager, I don't want her to come round to see me necessarily, but as a manager she should have contacted me. She doesn't know if I need anything or if everything is OK. And I then received a letter last week form HR – I know my HR manager – requesting a meeting to discuss the long term. That communication to me is very impersonal, very cold, and again I am going to do something about that actually. I have to get over it. If I didn't have family and I needed support, there would have been none, obviously.

Veronica understands there is a context to this, a hospice which is extremely well resourced and a National Health Service which is increasingly stretched in terms of time and resources. She knows why and how simply being such a vast organization as the health service can lead to such instances of inconsiderate behaviour. But as a personal experience, she found it deeply hurtful.

Veronica has felt well supported by most of her family and friends. She has good long chats on the phone with her brother in the United States. She is used to having long chats with friends when she came home from dropping the kids off at school, and they make a cup of coffee and natter for an hour or more. She has never felt particularly inclined to use social media or computers, though she is happy to share jokes or photos once in a while and she found creating a standard text message alleviated the burden of repetition in keeping people informed about her prognosis. She appreciates supportive texts from people who don't have time to phone, but, to be honest,

she much prefers to receive cards, which are far more meaningful to her: 'I love cards.' There is also all the practical help,
which means her freezer is always full of meals when she is
undergoing chemotherapy.

I've got a friend who I've known since I was five. She's like my
sister. She is absolutely my 'bestest' friend. Been there for me
through thick and thin. There, when I had both children. A very
busy lady. And it's very difficult for me to see her. But when I've
needed her in the treatment, she was there. And I've got another
friend as well that I've been friends with since I trained, and she's
been the same as well. Those two friends have been amazing.
They've been over nearly every week since I was ill. They're like
family really. My mother I talk with most days on the phone.
Maybe every other day; she'd like to talk every day. I try and
ring them. My father unfortunately is very deaf. They are very fit
though, at 87 and 82. My dad drives up here sometimes. So telephone really. Because they haven't been up a lot to see me. My
house is so small. Being ill it's difficult to put them up really.

Yet within that circle of support, there is a kind of hole at
the centre – her husband, but also to a degree her son. Maybe
it is the men, in particular, who just find it difficult to even talk
about it. Perhaps men are more embarrassed by breast cancer, in
particular. Men found her reaction, even her positivity, difficult
to cope with. They are not people who like to share intimate
things and they were clearly very uncomfortable with her own
openness.

My husband is a funny kettle of fish really, not the most sociable of people. He doesn't find it easy to talk to people. He's not

a conversationalist. Even with me, really. And it is quite difficult now. He does insist on me ringing him every morning, to make sure I'm still alive. Just wants me to say hello, I'm fine; very short on the telephone. He would ring me every day from work. I think if you met him you'd see he does have a communication problem. Been a bit of a problem since I've been ill, really, because I've had a lot of people around. I think it's helped him realize how many people there are for me. He wouldn't sit there; he'd sit for a little bit and go upstairs. I'm the social one. Been married 18 years this year. It's been difficult. Particularly since I've been ill as well, I think. When you have a life-changing experience, it doesn't make things any easier because we are very different, but I'm sure it's the same in a lot of marriages. My son is obsessed with the Xbox. I think it makes them unsociable. He's not unsociable with his friends, but trying to get children to come downstairs and sit and have a dinner . . . They just want to go upstairs and go onto their machines. I'd far rather he went out and saw his friends and did something. But he does go out, he's gone out now with his friends, so I shouldn't moan too much.

Perhaps this also helps explain Veronica's enthusiasm for the hospice as the 'Champneys for the terminal'. The difficulties Veronica feels when it comes to the people she expected to be at the centre of her care, her husband or her manager of 22 years, lead to a still greater appreciation of those who have clearly given sensitive consideration to the whole question of how to provide palliative care. In short, Veronica is in a very good position to appreciate why we need hospices and need to support them.

Story 3

The Curse of Confidentiality

One entirely unexpected result of this research was finding that a major cause of unnecessary suffering to hospice patients were regulations that were intended to benefit them: the rules around ethics and confidentiality for patients' medical records. The clearest indictment of this state of affairs came from Marilyn.

Born in 1960 and a bit of an activist, Marilyn was rather more forthright than most about her experiences since being diagnosed with breast cancer. The first thing that struck her was the degree of letter writing.

It came as more of a surprise to me that you [Maria] would send me a letter, which is wasteful, from an environmental point of view. If someone sends you a letter saying can you come on Tuesday at six, you look at your diary and say no, but I could do it at five, but I'm not going to send a letter back saying I could do it at five. The phone would be much easier. I found it old fashioned. I expect to get letters from hospitals because I think when you make an appointment with a hospital, it will be in a month's time and you understand their clinic days are certain days, so if you see them it's always going to be a Thursday. When I was trying to meet with you, I had rung up and said, 'Is there someone I can see?' And they said 'Yes, you should talk to Maria.' You and me, only two of us trying to make an appointment. I thought it was a given that you've got a diary and I've got a diary that's got things in it. Much more sensible to speak.

But in truth this was a pretty minor matter. It was another issue that had really got Marilyn's goat.

I think I stand on complete openness of record sharing between professionals. Because I feel that at the moment it's incumbent on me to be very well informed and educated about my own condition and my own history. Because you can't expect that new medical people that you see will understand all of that. For me, I feel I'm in the middle of this – joining up the dots. It would be a relief, I think, to know that that information was accessible to all parties. When I go to the breast clinic, I have one file, and when I see an oncologist, there's another file. That's not taking into account anyone I might see here, or my GP, or the guys I had the surgery with. I know there are files about me all over the place, but they only show one aspect of my story. I feel I have to be a sort of safety net. The problem with that is to make sure that they don't miss something. If those guys over there don't know I've had this thing over here, then they might do something that wouldn't be a good thing. But, because I'm not medically trained, I don't have the knowledge to know about such things. Yet it's down to me.

It would be a relief to feel that you didn't have to do that because I do worry. I don't really understand the impact of thing this and thing that. I can try and educate myself about it, but it's quite hard to penetrate medical information or whatever. There is a sort of responsibility that it would be nice not to have. I don't think it affects my everyday well-being but when it comes to interactions with medical people or people who provide support for me, then, yes, it does affect it.

Marilyn could just about imagine herself as the conduit, ensuring that each medical professional she saw was appraised of what had happened with the others. But it was obvious that there was no way her elderly father could occupy that role, so for him this lack of exchange of information was serious and dangerous.

I suppose for me what is at the heart of this is, as the patient, you want to survive your disease if possible and be treated effectively. That has to be, you know, there has to be information available to the people who need it. I think it's OK when you're competent and compos mentis and not ill. The problem is that when you become ill and you're not quite so capable, it's much harder to keep track of all of this. So, my dad, he's not capable of managing all that data that he needs to manage.

Recently, Marilyn has been appalled by a story told by one of her friends who lived in Lancashire regarding the death of her husband. There were just too many different people involved.

A night-duty nurse would stay during the night, a district nurse would come once a day to review the drugs, care assistants would come and wash him and change his clothes. The latter were provided by a plethora of different agencies with fancy names. The third night, there was no district duty nurse. Instead, a private nursing agency was providing someone to spend the night.

Apparently, a personable young man arrived dressed in a suit and carrying a laptop, who had then explained that he was the son of the owners of the agency providing emergency help. During the day, he was training to be an accountant.

She too has had quite a few carers.

Got your breast-care nurses, supposed to be coordinators. Do quite a good job of that, but couldn't answer any questions on the side effects. Then you've got your surgeon, she's very nice, but I only really speak to her when I see her. Then you've got your oncology team. Then I saw a different sort of oncology team. I had a DVT in my arm; I have to speak to them about anything like that. But mostly now I call the oncology team, but you just phone a number. You want to speak to a doctor, but the doctors are always busy so you get to a chemotherapy nurse, and they are very, very good, these nurses, but they are not doctors. I can't quite work out the best way to speak to a doctor. It takes you ages just to get through to the receptionist. They want to know if you've got a temperature, and it's just like, no, I've got a side effect, I don't want to discuss it with you. End up speaking to the nurse. Nurse says she'll speak to the doctor, doctor will get back to you and then in a couple of days they probably will. But, yes, if you're out of hours, you phone a special out-of-hours number. I have sometimes not been given the best advice. When I had the DVT, that of course is an emergency, and I just can't find any way of getting hold of anybody in an emergency, and I suppose I should have gone to A and E [accident and emergency] but they [her own doctors] knew all the treatment I'd had, so I didn't really want to go to A and E, but I knew somebody that had helped me. I just phoned her number and she managed to sort me out. I was OK.

I think communication with hospitals can be very difficult. The nurse would tell others to speak to the oncology doctors. She wouldn't communicate it for me. Which I would have to do then, if I could get hold of them. I mean you can, it's just not easy and, when you are not well, you want things to be easy. I think it's so difficult for people. And I'm not frightened of hospitals either. I don't hold them in awe. I don't hold doctors in awe. I just think of them as people; they do something that I can't do. The GPs don't want to be emailed either. I mean, I can order prescriptions online. That's quite good that we can do that now.

I'm quite scientifically minded, really. It just became the most important thing in my life. I gave it that perspective really, that priority. I didn't give advice to anyone. Some people just don't want that; got to be quite careful about pushing your own view of things because everybody wants to deal with these things in their own way. I'm a bit cautious. I would always advise some- one to go to the best centre to be treated. That would be the first thing I'd say. But if people turn round to me and say no, it's just as good locally, and I want to be treated locally, I'd go, 'It's OK, then.' Find out as much as you can about the treatments. Don't think too much about convenience because there is nothing more inconvenient than dying. And then, anything you want to know, don't be frightened to push to find out. If you really get stuck, go to your GP. And I'd like not to think I was a pain in the neck. So I suppose it's giving it priority, taking it seriously. I wouldn't say I don't trust the doctors. I do trust them to a large extent, but I don't just leave it up to other people. The person who cares the most about you is you. You will put more effort into this than anyone else. Don't just put your head in the sand and allow it all to happen. They've got a lot of people to worry about; you're not the only one. Put everything you've got into this and, if it goes wrong, there was nothing else you could have done. That would be my advice.

Around the same time that we were talking to Marilyn, I had started to interview a sample of 20 hospice staff to get their side of the picture. They strongly affirmed Marilyn's representation of these problems. They knew only too well that a patient assumes that all those who visit and see them in a capacity of professional medical care will communicate with each other. If a patient tells a medical staff member about some new symptom, or their treatment preferences, or some other significant detail, they think that they have thereby informed all those people that they are dealing with. They are not expecting to repeat every piece of information to every different person they see. What is clear is that unfortunately they cannot make these assumptions. The staff explained that there are several reasons for this.

Firstly, there is the sheer number and diversity of those involved. A patient in an end-of-life situation is likely to encounter an oncologist, their local GP, the local hospice staff, a hospice-at-home facility, a Marie Curie or Macmillan nurse, a district nurse, a local hospital and social carers. If they use private health care, or have some complications in their medical condition, such complications can multiply. The number of people visiting tends to rise as the illness progresses with patients desperately trying to keep track of a bewildering array of individuals and appointments by scribbling on calendars on walls or next to their beds.

Much of this is inevitable and the services offered are often complementary and vital; for example, the hospice that takes in-patients is separate from the service that supplies night care at home, but both are needed. But in addition every single member of staff could recall situations where a patient's welfare has been significantly impacted by the failure of carers to exchange information about patients. Finding out a patient's medical history could become a kind of detective work based on a creakingly old system of letter writing and faxes. As a hospice doctor put it, 'So I will see a letter and there is a cc to •••• Hospital and I will say "Why were you there?" And they will say "to see the diabetics team", and I am like, "Oh, so you're diabetic."' Knowing about diabetes is crucial for a doctor prescribing medication.

Hospice staff had many, many stories about requests they themselves had made for basic information about patients that were refused by a wide variety of institutions, ranging from GP surgeries, to hospitals to X-ray departments. An example was a palliative nurse working at weekends to cover patients from another palliative team, who was not allowed to access the records of these same patients. Doctors talked of routinely having to administer to patients without having been allowed access to those patient's medical records, noting that not only does this destroy their reputation with patients, but it has inevitable consequences for inappropriate diagnosis and treatment.

By contrast, not one single member of staff could recall an instance where a patient had suffered significantly because of a breach of confidentiality in the use of media communications to share medical information between professionals. Such breaches of confidentiality that did occur were inevitably verbal, such as gossip or discussion of patient records when in the presence of a relative. But, even then, the fact that an inappropriate person gleaned some information the patient would prefer to have kept private was not, in itself, a cause of the kind of pain, suffering and failure in appropriate care that results from the lack of information exchange. It was always quite trivial by comparison.

The underlying cause of this problem is immediately evident when speaking to junior staff, who discuss the issue of confidentiality as one of personal fear. They fully believe that an infringement of these regulations about confidentiality of patient records could lead to the loss of their jobs, even without significant negative impacts upon patients. By contrast, no one suggested that a failure to share information about a patient would lead to a loss of their jobs, even when this has had serious consequences for a patient. They often talked about confidentiality of patient records being drummed into them. The upshot of all this is a climate of fear which seemed to be the main reason that almost all junior staff believe that the use of new media is prohibited, even though they have never seen evidence that such prohibitions actually exist. One suggested that the root of all this was money, a belief that institutions could be more easily taken to court for breaches of confidentiality than for retaining confidentiality.

This blockage on data also applies to senior staff. As a hospice doctor noted, 'It's a nightmare getting things like scan results or blood test results. We have to rant and rave.' A typical example given by a doctor was the following:

Last week we needed the results of a CT scan. So, in order to get this, J had to ring the GP surgery and ask them. Then wait because they have to ring her back to prove it was her. Then wait again because they need to give her a fax number so she could in turn send a letter to request the scan. I needed that information at 10.00 in the morning, not at 4.00 in the afternoon, which meant I couldn't do anything till the next day. Which meant the patient lost 24 hours.

She concluded, 'Confidentiality is important but the key point is the patient. We are all in medicine to help care for patients and make them better, and the moment when the process starts becoming a danger to them, we have lost sight of things.'

Marilyn felt, much as did the nurses and the doctors, that this obsession with ethics and confidentiality was part of a wider issue of conservatism in the health service that was also reflected in their general use of media.

I think that's maybe how their system is designed and they are frightened of emails flowing about. Can they keep track of who said what to whom? Maybe they feel the whole system has to be properly changed. You have to phone up, and they're not there, they phone you back. But if you could just email them, it would go to the person who needed to answer it. I don't want to be told by email that I've got breast cancer. But I want to be able to email them saying these are my issues, and if they felt a phone call was necessary, then I would find this useful. It's quite hard to communicate with hospitals, hard to get through to the right people. It puts you off doing it.

One of the most absurd consequences of this conservatism with regard to confidentiality has become the retention of the fax machine as a primary means of communication between hospices and various NHS institutions. The fax is testament to the negative effects of this cult of ethics and confidentiality upon actual media usage. In practice, all staff regard the fax as the least safe, least reliable and least efficient means of communication. One member of the hospice staff calculated that perhaps 10 per cent of her time was used in trying to fax. This was partly because of the unreliability of these machines, which involves feeding them, checking all documents have gone through, not knowing if they have been received in full, etc. The fax is also regarded as notoriously unreliable, often going to the wrong person and being received in a place where it can be seen by someone other than the intended recipient. Rules about the siting of fax machines are routinely flouted. A doctor stated, 'Sometimes you even have to block [the patient's] name out, and you are just hoping it's the right person that's picking it up.' Interviews provided a veritable deluge of anti-fax stories and frustrations. Compared to the fax, new media, such as email and texting, seem to be models of reliability and precision, targeting precisely the intended recipient. Yet at the time of this research, ethics and confidentiality rules stipulated the use of the fax. As one doctor suggested, 'the fact that GPs, without regard or question, accept a life of faxes and letters in work practice that they would consider anachronistic and inane in their private life was in some measure a sign of an exotic culture or devoted adherence to custom that would be of interest to an anthropologist.' That doctor was right.

Story 4

Parkinson's

In a book whose topic is hospice patients, we need to confront the experiences of frailty and a loss of communication that no new media can remedy. Doris, a retired clerk, and her husband Herbert, a retired teacher, are in their eighties. Although Doris, who has Parkinson's, is unable to make use of any new technology directly, it is her husband's use of the internet, along with paid housekeepers, that keep them connected with the outside world.

Herbert explained:

Herbert: Doris can't communicate in any way. We had someone from the hospital neurological department, as part of the charity set up by Stephen Hawkins, and they came here and tried various things for Doris so she could get on with the phone and the TV. And you couldn't cope with any of it, could you? They did try very hard. Doris can't connect; she can't talk very much. You can hear: she's very slow, got to take things in. I mean, really, she's completely out of touch unless it's me and the carers. Even I find it hard to hear Doris; her voice is going all the time. That's the Parkinson's; it's fading away. She has to say things two or three times. Getting harder and harder. When we speak to our daughter, which I do every week, I sit alongside Doris so she can hear everything and put in an occasional word. Before we start, she reminds me of anything she wants to say to her. But when it actually comes to talking to people on the phone, Doris finds it very hard because there's such a long time while she reorders her thoughts and gets it through to her mouth, and of course it's sad on the phone. People think she's gone away or the phone has gone dead or something.

Since we've been in retirement, a lot of the time has been spent bringing up our grandchildren. Two of the families lived here; we spent a lot of time bringing them up, didn't we? My son and his daughter, my youngest daughter and her husband were not very domesticated – had a lot bringing those up, didn't we? But Doris was diagnosed when she was 65, something like that. Diagnosed by the man examining her hand. Doris was learning the piano and suddenly she couldn't play it, went to a specialist to see her hands and he said you've got Parkinson's, which was a bit of a blow. Not the subtlest way of telling you. We used to go swimming. Doris is a very good swimmer, then she found she couldn't float. Slowly started sinking.

We're always busy. Had 15 visitors in the past two days. Carers, window cleaners, chap who helps to do the garden, four grandchildren, two children. A visitor who comes from the hospice, lovely woman that comes in and reads to Doris. We've noticed that, over the years, once you get to know everyone, nobody moves from the lane. We've got to know virtually everyone in the lane, but it's not what you'd call a close community. Send Christmas cards to each other, speak to each other, meet them in the lane, one or two people that come in and see you two or three times a year. It's class as well. Everyone on this lane has to have a lot of money to live here. Accountants, managing directors – the house in the lanes, the last one, went for a million. We are here. We had a big piece of land in ••••. We'd sold up to a builder and we had the cash to pay for it; we got it very cheap. Normally, we wouldn't have bought a house in this road, out of our range; this was right at the top of our capability. I was brought up in a working-class cul-de-sac, then everyone knew everyone's business. That was a different era as well. But Doris grew up in an area like this. Comes from a slightly higher background to me.

We weren't joiners. We weren't anti-social but our life was just so full. I've got several cousins around. I'm very interested in family history, people who have gone to America and all sorts, that's quite strong with me. When you're teaching all day, you're dealing with people all day. And you don't feel very friendly, just having to deal with other people. Don't want to talk; in actual fact, you're using up a great deal of psychic energy from talking. I still write letters. Last one I wrote was about three days ago. A boy that was in the same cul-de-sac. I've kept in contact with people from all through my life really. Being artistic, I have a peculiar kind of interest, which most other people don't. In fact, I find most other people are blind, don't look at pictures or anything like that. So when you come across someone who's interested in that kind of thing, you tend to make friends with them and keep in contact although they move further away.

Largely this has migrated to the computer; so much easier. I do occasionally send images, but I tend not to. I write a great deal now. I'm cooperating with someone writing a biography of Doris's father. So I use the computer all the time to send him files and things on the letters I've got and that sort of thing. He'll bring this book out. Doris's uncle was killed in the war. He has already written a biography of him. And this is a second biography; two brothers, you see. We met Doris's father . . . why I am I doing all the talking? Am I offending you?

Doris (slowly): No, you certainly don't, ever. Fact is, I have a strong creative drive, too. And I've written stories and poems. Father was a sailor in the First World War. To write, I could use a computer, but my hands are . . . I can't do it on any old computer, I need a program. I did consider it, decided against it; just too complicated, in my view. I'd rather, I don't know, how did I proceed from there?

Herbert: Since Christmas, we've spent time going through all Doris's old poems and putting them in order. It was nice that she can still deal with all that. Got a lot of booklets, haven't you? Got masses of them.

Doris: Categorized them under subject matter.

Herbert: Your worst thing is you can't draw and write any more. We get up at 7 a.m. and go through to 9 p.m. and we're busy all the time. Watch virtually no television. Watch *Neighbours* for half an hour, don't you? When I make tea. But as you say, audio. But we listen to radio a lot. Radio 4, don't we? Typical day . . .

Doris: Slight differences.

Herbert: I wake up about 7.45, get up and open up the house. Carer comes at 8 and she's here for three hours. Got four carers, pay for them all. Not an agency. Both our children married abroad, and then one of them divorced and married a Slovakian. And she has organized it all. Head of the local mafia of Slovakians. I kid you not, she's arranged for all of them to come. And they are very, very good. So well educated, they are working well behind the pay grade or whatever it is. And they are extremely good. And they are so careful. And they haven't got this business about being servants, which the English have got. They are lovely, aren't they, and such good companions for Doris. Part of the deal was they would be good companions. We weren't just hiring them as carers, but they have to be able to talk to Doris, which they do. There's our carer getting married; she invited us to her wedding. Beautiful lady. She's been coming to us for three years. She organizes the others. They are all the same, very well educated, very sensitive, aren't they? We did have local people to start with. They were dreadful, absolutely dreadful. It was dreadful. Had them for one month, had 15 different carers. Some turned up and couldn't speak English, were here for 20 minutes, what on earth could you do? Explain about Parkinson's – how do you do that to someone from . . . ? Now we have four ladies who have got a monthly rota they worked out amongst themselves. Three hours in the morning and two hours in the evening. Just started last week. I went up to the doctor and she told me if I didn't get more help I'd be cracking up. Because it's very, very hard work, isn't it? We pay £13 an hour. Went to the local agency and they were charging £16 an hour. When they started with us, they wanted £12.50. I pay them £13 now. I always give them a bonus. That's the agreed amount. And we pay them extra for Sundays as well. But they are very good, they really are.

I do everything online. All the food comes online. All the shopping. The same with the doctor – sends in a prescription and it's delivered from the chemist. If it wasn't for the net, we should have had to move from this house without any doubt at all. I sold the car as soon as, soon after I retired about ten years ago. It was getting so expensive and I can't take Doris out very much. She goes off to sleep. So we weren't using it, worked out it would be cheaper with taxis, and it is. But it does mean I have to call on my children occasionally, or the carers, to take us to hospital. But it's only about once a month I call on someone to take me to the shops or something. But if the line goes down, don't know what we'll do.

I taught a lot of children and I should think 40 or 50 of them have actually been in contact. I was 22 years in the same school. It was a lovely warm school, the children were very friendly. They still come and visit us some of the children, don't they? Yes. Eusebia is a doctor now; we went to her wedding. No, I went a couple of years ago. A lot of immigrants – they were a joy to teach, whatever people say about them. It's like these Slovakians, they are just lovely people. Nicer than the English. You do share their lives like that.

The children keep coming in with iPads and saying you should get one of these and they show it to you and you say yes, yes. But it's not on. Doris couldn't use it. I honestly don't have any time. I know it seems extraordinary to say but I have no time at all to myself. I mean, I don't want to be a moan about having to work hard, but I'm just trying to tell you how it is really. I know the hospital carers are always on at me but I'm afraid of the internet for medical information. I avoid it to be honest. And I do avoid the Parkinson's stuff.

Doris: You're a recluse, aren't you?

Herbert: It's difficult with the Parkinson's. I have to deal with the pragmatic side of it. I don't want to hear all that might go wrong or I shall start looking for it. It's a bit of a cowardly way, I leave it to the doctors to deal with. It's hard enough to cope with anyway. That Doris has got it, without having to . . .

Instead, I look up the arts on the internet. I'll go into the National Gallery or Tate, V&A. I do that quite often. I've seen a bit of Google art. I don't have time for browsing. I'm a bit of a workaholic. I've set myself projects to do all the time, always got two or three projects. So if I've got any spare time I give it to that; my own art projects. I do a lot of drawing and printing, projects a bit like Doris's father's biography, family history. Doing some research for my cousin at the moment, who's just had her half-sister turn up and she's 65 years old; didn't know she existed! That was two days ago and I've been researching that straight away. She's in America. And it all happened before they emigrated; her father had a child that she didn't know anything about. It is absolutely fascinating. I use that for research, but that's what I'm researching at the moment, trying to find out if this woman . . . want to know if she's kosher, not after any money. I'm the only one with any memory of her father when he was here.

Doris: I had one sister who died about three years ago. Nieces and nephews, yes. She had two boys. There is a family down the road. A daughter died. In her forties. Her mother was very pleased with the hospice care.

Herbert: She praised you [the hospice] up to the nines. Our first contact, just trying to recall, it came from the Parkinson's nurse. We talked about what Doris was going to do. Got quite bad, and whether she was going to go into a home or die at home. We spoke to the doctor about it, and Doris wants to die at home. And then they suggested that we came to see the hospice. And when we were there, we'd learned that you had outside as well as inside care. Which seemed a very attractive thing to me, and that's really how we got onto it.

Story 5

Four Friends

The following two, otherwise highly contrasting, stories focus on the role of close friendship as a huge element in the life of some terminal patients although, as this book progresses, we will see why such friendship cannot be taken for granted. The 'four girlfriends' has become something of a cliché in television serials. The story of Chrissie, who is in her forties, suggests, however, that this genre is not entirely without foundation.

Chrissie was born in Leeds and came to the village to be with her husband who had lived in the region since he was seven. They have two grown-up sons. She worked as an assistant in a GP surgery and was especially good at helping patients who were nervous, giving them a sense of calm, which she enjoyed. She had tried nursing but hated it. Chrissie would like to be working now, but her cancer is quite severe, affecting her spine, and she knows she will not work again.

The last 18 months was a bit of a shock. It's not like working up to retirement. It's sudden, almost overnight. One day I was OK, fit and healthy, the next I was flat in bed and then in hospital. Very quick. All went from there really. My very close friends . . . there's four of us altogether. We all met at antenatal class. It was a classic friendship. The antenatal clinic is not there now. There was one in the community centre. We all arranged to meet up after we'd had the babies. We made a pact never to talk about babies, nappies. We talked about clothes, going out, anything but babies. Had had enough by then. It's the easy subject. It's what you've all got in common. We're all in the village. Walking distance. We all meet up. We try to see each other about once a week in the evening. Maybe more often in the afternoon if people aren't working. We go to each other's houses. The husbands know each other as well. Can go out for a drink or a meal, or the girls will go out as the girls. Last time we went out, we went to ••••. Or go for lunch on a Saturday . . . went to Jamie Oliver's restaurant in ••••. That was nice. Guys do their own thing. Then sometimes we'll . . . like, they came round here one Friday night. All the men came. Kids, no, they're not friends. They've all grown up and dispersed really. We're all kind of still left here.

When I wasn't well, I was bed bound for six months. Couldn't get out of bed. Massive, yeah. It was very difficult. My eldest son worked from home so he could be with me during the day. And my husband was brilliant, you know, but he had to go out to work. He did everything at the weekend. The girls were fantastic; brought us closer. My three good friends came round every other night, really. I mean they were fantastic, just fantastic. If I'd have asked them to do anything, they would have done it. But I didn't because my sons would do stuff, so they didn't need to. They used to bring me things when they came to see me, little things. And the girls from work, they were brilliant. Filled a big picnic basket. Everybody brought something. Put it in this basket. And somebody brought it round. I'm still working through it. We are all excep-tionally lucky, the four of us. You don't talk to many groups of women who are as close as we are. We are very, very close. I don't know, you could say stars were all aligned when we first met, who knows. Because I've known groups of girls at primary school . . . it's been awful really. They've called each other friends but one's walked away from the group and the others are all talking about her and it's like – oh, I'd rather be on my own than be in a group like that.

I had to have a stem cell transplant. And, I mean, I was just not fit to do anything for a couple of weeks. My husband used to ring the girls and tell them what was going on so they could tell other people. And when I was first diagnosed they were the people I told before everyone else knew. You kind of filter it down, as it gets into your own head. Was a massive shock really, almost like you're talking about someone else. So you tell a few people at a time. Sometimes they used to take me for my hospital appointments, scans, X-rays, whatever I needed. They used to come and collect me. One works from home; she does hairdressing. Another one is a chief executive of a third world charity, full time. But she could do a bit of flexi time. And another one is a work training assistant so she's at work full time as well. I just think it was . . . I know you can say the word 'luck', but what is luck, really? I think it was a meeting that you might only get once in a lifetime of four people who are on the same level, understand each other and don't judge people, don't judge each other.

Now we all have a child of 26, first child for two and the second for the other two. We were all pregnant at the same time, having cravings together. We all stayed in the village. Might have had something to do with it. I think you're more inclined to move if you don't get to know people in your area. If we had just moved here and I was on my own during the day, then possibly you would like to go to things like the village choir or amateur dramatics to meet people. But you don't feel as if you need to when you're in this situation really. I know it sounds a bit miserable, really.

It kind of confronts people with their own mortality when someone they know very well is hit with something like this. Makes them take a step back, makes them say thank God it's someone else and not me because I'd think the same thing. It draws you closer in together I think. One of my friends had bowel cancer. I think actually she was worse than me. She ended up with a colostomy. She was devastated, really devastated. But like you quite rightly said, because I was working in a GP unit, I was more used to it than she was. She'd never seen anything like that, had never had to deal with anything like that. I think, with me, I was more matter of fact about it. She was, you know, in a real state about it, which I can understand. She never got used to it, she had it for six months. And she was back at the consultants pleading with him to reverse it every other week. And eventually she did have it reversed. You can. She's fine now. Thank goodness.

I can understand why people go to pieces. Cancer, it's a big deal. Life-threatening thing. But I think: don't dwell on it, don't be a patient. I'm very intolerant [laughs]. The three of us, when she was in hospital, we used to go down every night. Used to give her a shower, change her and help her because she felt more comfortable than having other people do it. Then we looked after her when she came home. That was about three years ago now. Yes, we're very close. My husband thinks it's great. He never really thought about it until I started being ill. Saw the support that came and he was just, you know, he was amazed, really. Men are very different aren't they? Men have got this macho thing like – oh, you can't show that you care. I don't know: it depends on the man. I think if you get four exceptional men, then possibly, but I think probably not. I can't imagine the same thing with men, showering each other. We're all down to earth, matter of fact. She was in hospital for two or three weeks and we made sure she was never on her own. Would take it in turns to go and sit with her. She'd just lie there with her eyes closed and we'd hold her hand. Just to let her know we were there. In case she needed us. We are closer than some sisters. You can choose your friends; can't choose your family.

Don't have brothers or sisters. My mother is still alive. She's 91. My dad died about 25 years ago. She lives round the corner. After my dad died, we brought her down because there was nobody really. She lives on her own, little house, happy and healthy. She does like the village. I think she misses the north a bit, very much entrenched in the north. But she's settled, really. I think it will be about 22 years since she's been down here. She's not a great socializer. I mean, she just doesn't bother, happy with her own company. My mother felt, as you might say, survivor's guilt. I'm her only child and I've got an incurable disease and she's 91 and fitter than I am. I think she felt a bit guilty about that really. But take her out, muddle along really. iPad? She won't use anything – has a house phone. The four girls offered to do shopping or take her out or whatever she needed. But she's self-sufficient. She would go to the high street, fresh shopping. I take her now because I'm OK now to drive. But then, I mean, she had to get on with it, really. It's only 10–15 minutes to go up there.

It's – I dunno – some people can't cope with it and they turn away. A lot of people do that. I never found that. Not that I was aware of, no. Everybody – even people that I don't know very well, they were acquaintances – was getting my phone number off one of the three girls and ringing me and saying 'Anything you need, just let me know.' 'I'm going to the shops, do you want anything?' We know each other, but we don't socialize, we just say hello, how are you? But they all knew I was ill. Word got around, probably because they hadn't seen me for so long, and people come over, say 'How are you? It's nice to see you. How are things?' I think people don't want to ask. They know there's something but they don't want to ask because they don't know what to say really. We have conversations but we're not . . . we don't go into each other's houses. I think we did it once, one Christmas, Christmas drinks. But no, we wouldn't really. We're happy just to say 'Hello, how are you?' And that's it really. I know the man next door. He's elderly as well. Neighbours on the other side have just moved. Don't know them really. He's been round to do her garden but they wouldn't go into each other's houses.

Justine keeps trying to get me up to the hospice, and I keep saying Justine, no, I'm not interested. When I've had a hospital appointment, she'll ring me and find out how things went. I think also this makes a big difference; knowing a lot of people, you don't feel as if you have to go to these support groups. They are just so not for me. I don't wish to sit in a room full of people talking about the way cancer affected their lives. I know it sounds awful. I do not have a problem moving on. I didn't want to be ill in the first place. It's funny because some people who lived next door and moved to Wales came back a few months ago, and we went for a meal. She was saying to me, 'Can I get a friend of mine to ring you? She's had breast cancer and she'd like to talk to someone.' I'm just so not the right person to talk to. I said, yes, alright. I just thought I don't want to do this. I'm not a groupie person. I haven't got patience with people that wallow in illness. I'm the same person now. We go out and we don't talk about me being ill. I don't feel ill. I'm not going to be ill. When I was first diagnosed, the occupational health girl, she was great, but she was saying, oh, we'll put a rail here and we'll put this there. And I was like, hang on. Even if I can't get out of bed now, I am going to get out of this bed. And I don't want any rails, this that and the other. There's time for that in the future. Just don't want to sit in a room full of people commiserating with each other about how ill they are and what they've had done.

Justine mentioned a blog and I thought ok, I'll try it. So I went on there. I read all through this thing about this chap who's coping well. And then the next paragraph – this is so-and-so's brother: I'm sorry to inform you but he died last night. And then I was like – I'm really not interested. It's bad enough having it anyway. Just think, oh God, so painful and tiresome. You think, I want to get on with my life. Don't want to be dwelling on it, you know.

Story 6

Betty and Gloria

For a patient with a terminal diagnosis, just as at any other stage of life, sometimes what counts above all is having just one really good friend. When one is in one's eighties, and may have lost several friends, having this one strong bond may be even more important.

The only request we made to the hospice in terms of choosing patients for this study was that they were living in villages rather than towns so that I could compare them with my main ethnography in The Glades. Perhaps that is why the only people we encountered who were living in dedicated flats for the elderly were Betty and Gloria. The block where Betty and Gloria live has 26 flats, all occupied by widows, apart from three couples and three widowers. Though not related, Betty at 87 and Gloria at 77 spend much of their time together. Betty had had two children but one had died. She came to the village five years ago, following the death of her husband, in order to be near her son. Gloria had three children and six grandchildren but in truth she rarely saw two of her children, so again it was proximity to the one child whom she saw frequently that had brought her to the village, along with her sister and sister-in-law who were all living there.

Gloria still worked, at least a little. Her daughter:

comes here every morning between half seven, quarter to eight, to pick up the ironing she brought me the day before. She works for a rich lady, does her housework, and I do the ironing for her. I quite enjoy ironing. And sewing I like. I was a latchkey kid when I was a kid because my mum worked full time. Because she had to: during the war, they made women work, didn't they? And I didn't want my children to be like that. I wanted to be there for them when they got home from school. Which is what I did. And I just fit little jobs in that I could do.'

She still managed to find several kinds of work that allowed her to pick up her children after school at three, most recently as a cleaner in a local pub. Betty also had had several jobs, such as working in a sweet shop. They both left school at 14.

The flats have a few bespoke features:

Behind you is a pull cord, so if you need assistance or you're not well or anything, you pull it. When I press this one, the machine that looks like a tape recorder with a lightbulb, a voice comes through the machine. Because if I fell over there, how could I get over to that cord? There's one in the kitchen, bedroom, bathroom. It goes through Colchester, which is where the call centre is. They get in touch with the warden or they will ring the ambulance for you and bring the paramedics and that down.

This is the idea. In fact, the pull cord is tied up because otherwise Gloria finds her grandchildren play with it.

As is typical of working-class English people, there is hardly any visiting of each other's flats by residents, even at this age, despite their proximity and similarity of circumstance. Betty and Gloria talk of one woman who is quite open:

> She hasn't been here long and she's just lonely. Most of them, got a load of 90-year-olds here, and they're not my cup of tea, I don't mean to be nasty but I've got nothing in common with them. We've got a couple moved in before Christmas. The lady has Alzheimer's, can't walk or go anywhere, and the gentleman can't walk without his frame thing. They have carers in the morning, carers in the night, meals delivered to them, and they don't see a soul unless someone comes and visits them. And to me, they're in the wrong place. Because they're just getting worse. If they were in a proper place where they've got someone to care 24 hours. I'm not medical, but that's what my brain tells me, they need 24 hours. That's what annoys me about this place. Because they should have said, 'No, you can't come.' Because they need caring for, and there's no one to really care for them. They make a fuss, the daughter and that when she comes round, but she only comes round once a week, at the weekend. It's sad.

There are just two other flats in the block that they visit.

> You have to wait and see how the people in that block are getting on with them before you actually poke your nose in. You have to test the water before you get in. If we're all friends and someone isn't, well, then you call and take them something. But you can't push yourself onto people. To be honest, you can't like everybody. Some people you just don't like. Not that you ignore them, you say hello, but you just don't become friends with them.

Both have in their turn experienced a form of social exclusion. 'If you've been made a widow quite recently, and you've got friends and people you know around you who are couples, they're inclined to start gradually pushing you out. I think it's because you're on your own, you don't have a partner, and they feel embarrassed about having you around in their group. It always happens like that.'

As discussed in the conclusion to this volume, there is nothing new in this reticence with regard to visiting friends and neighbours. Much more surprising was the degree to which hospice patients sometimes show the same reticence with regard to their own family. On the one hand, both Betty and Gloria moved to the village precisely to be near to their children, but they then make sure to declare a certain distance, so as not to be a 'burden'. For example, Gloria's daughter assumed that she would join them for their Sunday lunch but:

> I said to her as I was moving in, one thing, I said, I am not coming to lunch every Sunday. And she looked at me. I said no, those three are getting bigger. They won't want me over here every Sunday. And they'll think we can't go because of Nan. And I said I should hate for them to think that. That's the understanding we have.

Precisely because Sunday lunch is an important family occasion, she doesn't want to intrude on the nuclear family.

On the other hand, their families show a strong commitment to keeping an eye out for them. The other day, there was a complete panic because unusually Betty and Gloria decided to take a walk down to the village since it was a nice sunny day.

And when I got back here there was a list of phone calls. My sister said, 'Where on earth have you been?' I said, 'Out for a walk.' She said, 'Good Lord – are you sure?' I said yeah. Apparently, my other sister had phoned her and said, 'I can't get any answer,' then my sister-in-law called and said, 'I can't get any answer.' So that was the panic.

Of course, Gloria has a mobile phone but, of course, she never remembers to take it with her when she goes out.

While the residents are reluctant to mix much in the private domain, they will happily meet in a public space. In particular, the local Baptist Church holds a weekly coffee morning. 'Majority of them do go. It's been dwindling off lately. We used to have about twenty come down, but this morning we only had about fourteen. Maybe not as many as that.' The church also organizes lunches and allows them to use the yard. The main problem of living in a village is that there is 'Nothing here. You can't go buy a lightbulb; nowhere to buy a dustpan and brush. Hardware shops? Get a bus. At the moment, we've got free bus passes so it's not a problem. Leaves about every 20 minutes or half hour. Tuesdays I go by car down to Sainsbury's. Go quarter past eight and I'm back by just after nine.' Neither attend church services much but they helped to choose the hymn for the harvest festival. They like the Baptist Church because it's modern, not like the traditional churches. On the other hand, one of those other churches does

the best Sunday lunch, called the Fellowship Lunch. They cook the most beautiful roast Sunday dinner for us. They do it every three months or so. And all the profits they make goes to good causes, to build wells in Africa or something like that. They send you back all the leaflets to show what they spend our money on. What they charge us, I think it's about £4, but we always put in more. So that's how they get their extra money to buy these things for the needy. They're so nice, they really are. And their children come, the young children, come and wait on us.

When in the flat, Gloria prefers to use her mobile phone rather than the landline since she can see more easily how much the call is costing her. Also, 'I text my son, my daughter, and any of the granddaughters and all that, family.' She also texts her daughter about whether there is ironing that day. In the case of her son, she has to text to find out if he is OK since he never picks up the phone. Mind you, she often doesn't answer the phone herself since she doesn't hear it ring. So it's just as well the family can text her. Gloria has a computer. She has never emailed but she does shop online, for instance buying football supporter shirts for her son's birthday or sending flowers to her daughter. 'I am on Facebook. I've even got a photo of me on it. Two of my granddaughters are Facebook mad. Everything that happens to them, they put it on Facebook. So I go have a look at them. Two daughters, my son, and my four grandchildren. All on Facebook.' It turns out that one other person in the flats and the warden are also on Facebook. She only looks at it about once a month.

Last time I think was when my daughter got her new dog. One of my granddaughters had to have her horse put down last week, and that's a bit upsetting. And that all goes on Facebook. She's got loads of friends. And I wouldn't put anything bad on there. I don't even know how to put a picture on there to be honest. Really, I think if you're going to have a computer, you need to have computer lessons. And I've never had lessons, only what my granddaughter showed me to do. Might send off for that thing. It comes on television sometimes, it's a magazine and it tells you how to use your computer, with words you understand. Not all these technical words. But I would be up for that.

The one television programme that quite a few people in the village watch is *The Jeremy Kyle Show* which follows the genre established by Jerry Springer in which people are goaded into having blistering rows with each other. It is this programme that has put Gloria off Facebook because 'It always comes up. It's on Facebook, and it puts me off. Causes all the arguments, affairs and they found out that another one slept with another one. This morning, I've forgotten what it's called, when they tell you who the baby's father is. They have a DNA test.'

Betty has been in touch with the hospice for around 18 months. Also:

> I went to the hospital and I stayed in for about five days, I think it was. And it was oozing blood and I took all the injections and stuff. And I must admit, if people complain about hospital, they don't know what they're talking about because they were so nice and the food was excellent and nothing was too much trouble for them.

Betty says that she saw district nurses, then a Macmillan nurse – however, patients often confuse hospice nurses with Macmillan. Currently, she sees a hospice nurse every Wednesday. 'She's very nice. She's lovely, isn't she? She doesn't talk to you as though you're stupid.' She wouldn't normally contact the nurse but she did recently when she found that the regime of pills she was taking was not stopping the pain. So the nurse doubled the dose. If Betty was feeling unwell, she would first consult Gloria, then the hospice nurse, who would tell her if she needed to see the doctor or anyone else. She has to go through the hospice reception in case the nurse is in a meeting at the time. But the nurse always returns the call as soon as she can. The nurse has also informed Betty about a hospice course for helping people deal with fatigue, which she then attended. 'If I find there's a time I have to go in there, I'm not frightened about going in.'

Just as Gloria is concerned not to overburden her family with her presence, so Betty is on a mission to protect her son from knowing too much about her illness. As Gloria puts it, 'They don't talk about the nitty gritty, about the illness. And you are such a good actress, Betty. He don't know whether he's coming or going sometimes. She don't want him to know too much, and he don't want her to know too much. Shielding each other.' Betty adds:

He says I don't tell him enough. What am I supposed to tell him? I don't want to upset him because I know he's got enough, going to work every day, his wife and the children, the house, and all this nonsense. To me, he's got enough worries. And I've never been one to moan about what's wrong with me. I've been a bit of a keep-it-inside person. I suppose I really shouldn't be like that, but then again I've always been like that, so it's going be hard to change. If it was really desperate, I mean sometimes I feel off, sometimes I feel all right. Today, I'm having a good day. He was going on holiday, so I didn't dare tell him I wasn't feeling well because I thought that'll put paid to the whole holiday and that's not fair. But he phoned me every night and I'm getting better and I said I'm fine now. And he said what do you mean, 'now'?

I mean, my daughter-in-law, I don't tell much; she's inclined to be a bit panicky. But I can hold what I call an intelligent conversation with my son. He says I don't think you're telling me the truth here, Mum. Why do you hide these worries from me? So now I'm getting into the habit of telling him. I'll tell him I'll be fine. I keep in touch more with my sister. I know it sounds silly but during the war we were always together. So therefore we somehow have got this extra little bond. And I can talk to her. But even she accuses me of keeping secrets.

Every week Betty phones her sister, her sister-in-law and a friend who lives in Oxford; occasionally she writes to them. That's really her circle these days. There were other friends, but they have all died. But closest of all is a new friend, one she only met when she came to live in the village – Gloria.

Story 7

Tom, Dick and Robin Rigby

Having read two stories about the positive contribution of friendship, we now face one of the most difficult findings of the study, which was the extent of the friendless. I am treating friendship as separate from family relations; for example, the patient within this story is married. For the Beatles, it was Eleanor Rigby. But in this study it was more often men who were the most isolated and lonely, and Robin was one of several who showed how much this resulted from a quite specific English sensibility.

Robin was born in London in 1927 but has lived in this rural lane since 1954. He retired at 65, having started with a good science degree from Cambridge but ended with a string of entrepreneurial ventures that tended to be only half successful and not especially enjoyable. An unemployed daughter lives not very far away, but an employed son is rather more distant. Robin was supposed to have been in contact with the hospice for over a year but the first time he had actually phoned them for help was the morning we came over. 'Bit of a muddle to get me up off the toilet.'

In fact, one of the curious things about Robin was how much

he disliked using the phone since most older people see it as preferable to other media.

> When you do these things by phone, one tends to get mixed up. They're thinking about something else and I'm thinking about what I'm thinking about. So somehow it doesn't click. You try to give some additional explanation and the telephone conversation goes on and you get around to what you want to talk about. So it can be extraordinarily complicated. But if you email someone, you hope that they're going to read it in detail. If I email the hospice nurse, I have no doubt that she reads what you send and reads it properly. When someone wants to talk to you about it, you might be a bit mixed up. I prefer emails. Other thing is you get time to sort your sentences out so they are in the right order. If I get one of my emails, I could explain it. On the phone very often it can take a while for people to catch on to what I'm talking about, or for me to catch on to what they're talking about. Maybe I think about things a bit faster than I should and I get overrun. I prefer to initiate an awkward conversation in writing rather than on the phone. In business, I had to be on the phone a lot, spent one's day time talking to people on the phone.

If there is one thing that drives Robin to complete distraction, it is unsolicited commercial phone calls.

Today, perhaps with relief, he barely needs to use the phone. It is mainly to talk to his daughter twice a week. 'Me, I'll say how are you? Have you got anything to say? No? Goodbye.' Then there is a cousin who lives somewhere in the west whom he very rarely speaks to. He has a brother in Scotland, but communication is sufficiently rare that he only remembers to mention him as an afterthought towards the end our discussion. The brother has MS now but was never much in communication, having joined a very austere Christian group decades ago. Other than that, he largely leaves phone calls to his wife. Then as we go through each different potential means of communication, we seem to end up at the same place. He tried webcam for a while, when his son was in the United States, but didn't find it particularly satisfying then and gave it up after his son returned.

Robin does still get the occasional letter, one from an old university friend with beautiful handwriting. There is another friend in France with whom Robin exchanges letters around twice a year. Then as he thinks about this for a while, he added a goddaughter in Australia, the mother of one of his late university friends and the wife of an ex-business partner they used to go on holiday with. None of these are at all frequent. Indeed, from his side, they simply represent variations on the single letter that he writes each year that can be individualized with a bit of editing. For the goddaughter who lives abroad and his son, there are occasional emails. He would have contacted his goddaughter more often

but my goddaughter's mother, whom we're very friendly with, if you phone her up, she won't talk. She's scared that she's running up a bill. Even though it's free, they got used to things in the old days when you had to pay a fortune for a transatlantic phone call. Even if you used Skype, she'd still think the same. No, some people are stuck in an earlier age of technology. I mean, I am – everyone is to some extent.

So having gone through the list, it seems that almost all his communication, apart from with his wife, is with his son when he 'comes around for Sunday lunch once a month and that saves a lot of bother. He lives with a partner who has two children by her previous husband.' As for the grandchildren, they 'come round for various occasions like Easter Day or Christmas Day. We don't really communicate with them when they're in London. They don't phone us unless there is a reason. We have a perfectly happy relationship; we don't wish to impose. If they need help, I'll go to any lengths to give it. But generally speaking we don't interfere.'

Even if we were not discussing media, Robin's sense of retrenchment would be obvious and is reflected in his location in a rural lane. Robin never intends to visit London again. 'First thing we notice about going to London is that after a day there we are absolutely exhausted, or should I say poisoned by the polluted air, and we are disinclined to go.' His last reason for visiting was a dentist who has now left the city, so there will be no more visits. The nearest town is pretty limited:

> So by and large it's much more convenient to order stuff on the internet. The other reason is you get a lot more choice. Even if John Lewis opened a branch locally, they have a sort of semi one in Waitrose. If you look at the household products that they sell, you'll find them under the John Lewis name. We have my groceries delivered occasionally; Sainsbury or Waitrose. My wife comes and sits beside me and I say, 'Do you want this? Do you want that?' Have a usual-items list, which covers everything you've ordered within the last 3–6 months, and you run through that and say do you want six of those, one of those? Occasionally I visit. I bought that TV by going to John Lewis, simply because I wanted to see the thing before I bought it.

These days, Robin rarely even goes to the local town and he has never visited the hospice. He has other reasons to use the computer. In particular, there is YouTube:

Just because when I'm interested in something, I can look it up. Someone mentions music. I want to look up an old recording I might know about to see if I got it right. Look at clips of other people, John McCormack for instance, pre-war opera singer. Irishman. Very famous light tenor. Might look at YouTube if I want to look something up, to investigate rather than watching it for pleasure.

Robin was one of those who confirmed the advantages of our methodology. Because we simply appeared to be discussing a sequence of media, it was not apparent to the patient that we might be interested in the issue of loneliness and isolation. We had no wish to make people uncomfortable by making this explicit. Subsequently, by examining the detail, one can see how few significant contacts were left using any medium. The same applies to people that Robin might see face to face. 'At one time, I knew everyone in the road, but as we get older and the people who've been here for years disappear for one reason or another, the number of people you know tends to diminish. I'd say we're not even on [greeting] terms with half of them.' There are three or four that Robin knows but it is once in a blue moon that anyone comes to have a cup of tea.

As it happens, in this instance Robin himself broaches the topic of isolation, not defensively but to espouse what he sees as the value that lies in privacy.

Some people are perpetual chatterers and entertainers, and we aren't. We got married in 1954 and wanted to have a house somewhere. This place looked so nice that we looked in this area and picked up this two-acre plot. It's possible for people in this area to socialize. Around the golf club. In this area, for the houses, a big draw is the golf, which I'm not into. I simply came here because I liked it. Brought up in London, getting away from things. It just that we liked it. I don't know why but we've never been very sociable people. I mean, my wife talks like crazy. We're private people. Don't go round courting visitors because I feel isolated at this time. I spend more time asleep than I used to. I find the computer more of an occupation. I tend to just respond to the stimuli of the day or the week. Use the television. We spend too much time watching television, watch the 6 o'clock news, local news. It goes off when we have dinner in the dining room, then goes on probably for a recorded film after that. Bit of luck, we get to bed after that. Sometimes my wife says, 'Oh, we have time to watch an episode of *Flog It*.' By that time, we are just about ready to climb upstairs.

Ultimately, there is only one contact other than his wife, the token phone calls with his daughter and the son's monthly visit that Robin seemed to have with any regularity. 'We have someone who helps with the gardening, does all the gardening in fact. Very difficult to maintain the garden.' As the details of this portrait are revealed, the same story unfolds around his wife. Her only real social contact is her hairdresser. 'If you say, "Well, why don't you skip that? Do it yourself," she says, "Oh no, I enjoy going to the hairdresser." And that's Tuesday about 4 p.m. regularly. And if she misses it, she feels deprived. No doubt about it.'

It was only when I went through these stories systematically that it became clear that the same thing was true of several other patients who are not included in this book. The social encounters that they had retained were commercially based.

Story 8

My Fair Lady

It will be apparent by now that many of the stories in this book are juxtaposed in order to reveal contrasts. Mostly, we are dealing with a spectrum from the unsociable to the gregarious, and these stories illustrate the range of experience as well as what is typical. Because the population of hospice patients is so homogeneous, an unusual region of 'home-counties' England with only a minimal presence of minorities, it was hard to avoid thinking in terms of what is now a kind of remnant, a rare non-cosmopolitan Englishness, even if there hadn't been the intention of contributing to a wider anthropological project. But, then, what is this Englishness, and what is typical? We met Celia at a time when we had confronted much loneliness and isolation. Frankly, so many stories, such as Robin's, made English people seem rather cold and aloof. Celia, in her eighties, helped restore a sense of balance, reminding us that we also encountered warmth and solicitude. She helped us appreciate that cold and warmth were not contradictory humours in the lifeblood of the English, but often arose from very different circumstances. If we are thinking in terms of typicality, then, to be honest, Robin was more typical of older males and Celia of older females.

Celia also helped to personalize and give me a profound respect for a statistic. Maria, alongside being an experienced hospice manager and therapist and now working on this project, was also responsible for organizing the hospice volunteers. She had mentioned that there were more than a thousand of these – all unpaid. There are quite a number of hospices in the region and it seems this one is not unusual. It is an extraordinary figure. Yet it is consistent with our findings. So many of the older English people we met either as patients or in the wider ethnography turned out to be, among other things, volunteer carers. They all quietly, without making a fuss or asking for praise, did things for other people.

In the case of Celia, volunteering was more or less the synopsis of her life story. She talked at some length about working for the Samaritans. As with volunteering for a hospice, this is rarely just a matter of stuffing envelopes and making tea. It is taking a huge responsibility and drawing upon significant reserves of emotional maturity because the people you encounter may be people who are thinking of committing suicide, or, by contrast, have no desire at all to die but have a terminal diagnosis.

A number of factors had influenced Celia to constantly volunteer, including issues in her own childhood. Initially, she was pretty much pushed into being a carer by her mother:

She had a bad back, and I had to look after my sisters. What she'd do – she'd be a very good-hearted mum . . . the boys next door, their mother had died, and she took it upon herself to make meals for them. And she did it for a week, and it got too much, so I had to do it. And her excuse would be she had a bad back, so she had to be in bed. So imagine that, me a 12-year-old. I had to make food not only for my father and sisters but the next-door neighbours as well. And she never wrote to the school to say. So the truant officer came around. My father was a bit shocked about that.

Later on:

Because I had a few friends whose children committed suicide, and the parents – I worked with them – and they had no idea that their child felt that bad. That was one of the reasons why I became a Samaritan because I can't imagine how awful, to be that unhappy, and no one to talk to about why you are feeling like that. And the effect it has on the parents as well. Because they're going to feel guilty all the rest of their lives, you know – why did my child kill themselves? What was wrong? Why didn't they talk to me? So I thought, if that was my child . . .

A lot of my girlfriends – schoolfriends – would be at my door at least once a week because they'd had a fight with their mothers. So I used to bring them in, feed them, give them a talk, and I used to say, 'Your mother did this because she cares about you.' And then I'd take them home. Or sometimes I would have them sleep here. Because I never wanted my children to be in the position of those children. That must be dreadful, to not have anyone that understands why you're doing what you're doing, how you're feeling so bad about things. I remember how bad I felt as a child.

Apart from the Samaritans, there was volunteer work for the Citizen's Advice Bureau. Celia was also the almoner for a masonic lodge distributing alms (charity) to those in need. Another time, she helped as a police visitor. The list goes on. It wasn't all volunteering. At one point, she was employed as an arts and crafts specialist at a psychiatric hospital, although even that came after initially doing the same job as a volunteer. Then she was a manager at a care-at-home-services company. Later on, after she thought she had retired, she was persuaded to work for an undertaker because the owner recognized that Celia had exactly the qualities for that post. None of this was ever allowed to impinge upon the care Celia saw as paramount – bringing up her own three children. So, for many years, other work or volunteering crept in around the perimeter of her determination to be the best mother she could be. In turn, the end to both this work and most of her volunteering came when she took on looking after a grandchild so that her daughter could continue working.

Perhaps the reason why Celia makes one think of volunteering in terms of beauty is also because of the way certain juxtapositions develop in her narrative. Listening to Celia, caring starts to emerge as a craft, something whose detail needs to be developed in a highly skilled and gradual manner to achieve its effect, how precisely to balance insistence and concern, the time you can give and its boundaries. To be a good volunteer requires patience, opportunism, reticence, firmness and always consideration. In Celia's narrative, whenever she wasn't crafting her care work, she worked in craft, originally as a milliner. Even for those who can't pretend to have ever paid much attention to the world of hats, they might just recall the exquisite hats on display in the film of *My Fair Lady*. So it's hats off to Celia when one hears that she had personally been involved in crafting those very hats.

Women are often shockingly generous in talking about men. When they see a man going through cancer and becoming a terminal patient, they regard it as a kind of dissonance. These men are so proud, so concerned to retain their dignity and image. They are incapable of asking for help or acknowledging it when it comes their way. They don't want to or they can't talk about 'it'. Everything is internalized and repressed but all to no avail, as illness brings about a deterioration in their appearance and speaks on their behalf. So their wives say that it shouldn't happen to them; that they cannot cope. But, to an outsider, it's hard to share such sympathy for the buttoned-up males, and harder still to agree that it is somehow more acceptable for disease and affliction to strike women who have spent a lifetime caring for others, possibly including their fathers, husbands and sons.

This reluctance to report a problem that might have been treated earlier is characteristic of men in general. It is self-destructive when a condition has reached a terminal state because a male patient has been reticent about going to their doctor to report a symptom. But there is no reason to acquiesce in this asymmetry of concern. Celia makes light of her own suffering while talking at great length about the indignities this had involved for a man she had helped, as though fate should have known better. It's only the odd phrase that reveals the level of her own personal distress, for example when she admits that she would have preferred dying to suffering the effects of chemotherapy. Soon the scale of that suffering is revealed by her frequent response that something 'wasn't very pleasant'.

Not surprisingly, given her age and experience, Celia prefers familiar forms of communication, face to face or a phone call, that have served her well and which she regards as personal and real. She doesn't particularly like computers and the internet. As she remarks, 'spam' is something she prefers to encounter in a sandwich. At the Samaritans, she came to know the internet as a source of fear: inappropriate medical information, overly violent games. She has relatives who insist on researching her cancer online. As a result, they sometimes need some persuading that she is actually still alive, since apparently 'she is not supposed to be'. Sometimes the internet seems to make people just a bit stupid. But needs must, and she has felt so dreadful with repeated chemotherapy that she has even resorted to a round-robin email sent to around twenty people about every three weeks, just to keep them updated with her news. It would be too exhausting to tell them each individually.

These round robins are quite effective, producing a flurry of responses, including requests to visit her. Typically, she receives about 15 emails and four regular phone calls a week. Sometimes people send her really funny emails just to cheer her up. As with many hospice patients, she isn't so fond of being told she is 'brave' when she is merely putting up with something she can't do anything about. There is also her Jamaican friend of 40 years' standing, who phones her twice a day and who is one of the eight long-term friends who have stayed in contact ever since they worked together at the psychiatric hospital. They used to have collective dinners at their respective homes, or at least the ones where the husbands didn't seem too unfriendly. As seems inevitable in English families, there are one or two relatives that even Celia can't stand and where contact is now completely lost, and Celia has better things to do while dying than bother with people who seem unredeemably nasty.

Celia has visitors on most days, besides her daughters, one of whom visits every evening. She loves the way the daughter who made such a mess when she lived at home and never cleaned up is now punctilious in sorting out Celia's mess when she comes round; given Celia's continued fondness for craft, this is sometimes no small feat. There are other reasons she depends on their visits. 'Every three days, when I need my patches – I can't put my own patches on, morphine patches, because they have to be on a smooth part of the body, and I haven't got a lot of those; it's all bone. So she finds a place, usually on my back, and it's very hard to put something on your own back.'

There is one thing not even her daughters can put right. Something that has really 'got' to Celia when most things don't. She knew that mostly people's hair would grow back after chemotherapy. But she had always assumed that it would be more or less the same kind of hair that you had before in terms of colour, texture and form. If you have had straight hair, you shouldn't now suddenly find yourself growing curly hair. That's just not you. It's especially an affront because most people routinely check themselves in a mirror. Getting older tends to be gradual, but confronting someone with different hair which is not a wig nor a perm, somehow that's just a bit unfair. Above the scalp should be, like below the belt, relatively sacrosanct. 'I feel like I am doing an impersonation . . . I look too much like my mother, and I don't want to look like my mother.' It was bad enough being bald for a period. 'And I feel sorry for bald-headed men because my head – I'm freezing! And it's awful.' But at least that was temporary; this weird new alien stuff on the top of her head – that's so much worse.

Her visitors range from those who live close by and those from various phases of her past. When her daughter was young, she befriended various waifs and strays. For example, there was one whose home life was very difficult and who would turn up regularly with a suitcase when she had quarreled extensively with her own mother. It is surprisingly common, substitute mothers that distraught school-age girls turn to in desperation because they just can't cope any more with the tensions in their own home, often of their own causing. Celia recalls times when she has literally cuddled them to sleep. Celia was the kind of person who would freely lend them money; it would always be returned eventually. Some of these waifs and strays remain in touch to this day.

After so many interviews where neighbours seem to be regarded as best avoided, especially when they know you are ill, finally Celia seems to inhabit something that approximates to our imagined ideal neighbourhood: a community of support. In this case, Celia's personality is not the only factor. As an anthropologist, I tend to favour cultural explanations over technical ones to account for people's behaviour. But after several projects in England, I have found something strongly predictive about streets. The friendlier ones are almost inevitably a cul-de-sac rather than a through road. I now expect people in a cul-de-sac to know the names of their neighbours. Celia notes that in the last few days she has benefited to the tune of one lemon drizzle cake, some chicken soup, some flowers, some cards and constant offers to do the shopping. Just recently there was a lovely planter which a neighbour left on the doorstep without a note. As it happens, while respecting the desire for anonymity as amongst the purist expression of generosity, Celia discovered who this was. But then in the past Celia has done the lot. She has mown their gardens, arranged a funeral, even helped to organize the double glazing for a neighbour who was suffering from the cold.

Yet, even for Celia, even in a cul-de-sac, there are those others. 'There's a few who can't face illness. So you don't see them very much: occasionally I bump into people, but it doesn't last. I can quite understand – it is something to be fearful of. It's like when somebody dies – they'll cross the road rather than talk to you. And I quite understand that. But I don't let it bother me.' As she puts it:

It's a reserve that the English have. And they can't stand people showing their emotions. That's the big thing. If someone starts to cry, people panic. You know – 'I shouldn't have said that because that's made them cry' – and that's why people don't talk to you when you've had a bereavement. They don't know what to say to you so the easiest thing is just to cross the road. That was one of the reasons why my friend the undertaker asked me to go and work for him.

Celia tells a haunting story of a close friend who had Hodgkin's disease. After the diagnosis, every single member of the family backed off, even her mother, father and sisters. The only people who were prepared to even mention the disease were her friends. The family only came back into the frame when the disease abated.

So Celia has seen the other side to volunteering, just as we have, but none of this detracts from who she is and what she does, and the need to pay respect to this unblemished altruism. We should also acknowledge the numbers of people in dire suffering who have benefited from that statistic of more than a thousand volunteers for a single hospice. It is perhaps especially sad to meet Celia in the days of her own suffering but, through telling her story, she has been able to regain a sense of what she is worth and the contribution she has made with her life. For us, it is an honour to have had the chance of meeting her while that is still possible.

Story 9

Maypole

Several of the stories in this book relate to a wider sociality than either friendship or kinship. Celia is one example, but the people she helped as a volunteer were largely unconnected to each other. By contrast, for a few, but only a few of the patients, there was a strong sense of community. But community can be understood in several different ways. It is likely that there are a dozen people such as a Gerald in any given village, but I doubt there are many more than that.

Talking with Gerald, now in his seventies, I couldn't help but have this image of a maypole, standing tall in the village green, with the villagers dancing around it. He was the support, the still centre of everything that went on. This was not because he wanted fame or attention but because of his sense that this was his responsibility, the task that fate has allotted him. Gerald learnt the meaning of hierarchy from holding a very senior position in a rather old-fashioned company, Cable and Wireless, and henceforth everything seems to have been viewed from his commanding position at the apex.

What is an English village? For Gerald, there is a clear core, which consists of five institutions: the church, the cricket club, the golf club, the Lions Club (though that could equally be Rotary or Kiwanis) and a relationship I was never entirely clear about to the Masonic movement that attracted retired but senior professional and business executives. This constitutes a circle because it is the same core group of people who circulate the key official positions in all of them. Despite the small size of the village, it includes people used to wielding considerable author-ity. Gerald was once responsible for thousands of more junior staff. There is an ex-chair of one of England's major public schools and another who ran one of the largest companies.

You look around and you can see who ran big businesses, not because they look like they ran big businesses, but if you say, 'We're looking for a treasurer', one of them will say, 'Well, you know, I'm a bit busy, but I'll take it on.' And you know jolly well which group of people that person will come from – and it will be true of any village you go to.

The same people sit on the parish council, the church council, become chairmen of the Lions or the golf club – they are people such as Gerald. In many of these villages, the Anglican Church is located at the highest point in the village and the Anglican vicar is expected to sit on the major committees, even though most of these have no particular tie to anything religious.

The next concentric circle consists of other village activi-ties, such as the amateur theatrical companies. The Church is here represented in a rather different manner. In this second circle, when people refer to 'the Church', they don't mean the Anglican Church alone, but a more ecumenical presence that includes the leaders of the Catholic, Methodist and Baptist Churches, who have drifted in from the periphery to form a

'Churches Together' movement. In Gerald's village, there is still an almoner, someone who runs the almshouses that help the sick and the poor. In this circle are the people who organize institutions such as the history society or the vegetable and produce fair, and those who run the Women's Institute. What it has in common with the inner circle is that while the people who circulate around these institutions are different from Gerald's circle, here too it is the same people you seem to see again and again, almost irrespective of which institution one is visiting. But in this case it is a rather larger set of people, more like two or three hundred. There is an unspoken but clear differentiation of gender. Gerald's wife would expect to serve at some stage as chair of the Women's Institute or perhaps the flower arranging, and she is central to this second circle. However, she would never have those inner-circle positions in relation to the Lions or the golf club which tend to be held by males.

The next circle outwards encompasses those who associate themselves with the more egalitarian village activities. This includes the football teams but also the pub darts or quiz teams and such like. Often involvement is related to life stages. A woman who has moved into the village, for example, starts to socialize within mother-and-toddler groups, then helps with the guides and scouts when her children are young, and subsequently the football clubs when they are teenagers. On retirement, she continues to work as a volunteer for charitable institutions, almost certainly these days including the hospice, perhaps working in the charity shop. Such people continue to serve at every stage, in some capacity or other. Gerald describes them as foot soldiers rather than the officer corps.

The final circle, and in many villages these days perhaps the largest of all by number, comprises those who do not get involved in anything whatsoever. They live there and their children might go to scouts or to play football weekly, but they pay no heed to who is actually organizing and ensuring that these things exist. They simply take them for granted and feel no sense of responsibility. One might assume these were typically the London commuters, but my larger research project showed that a surprisingly high percentage of those with no involvement at all in village activities are in fact born in the village or nearby and have always lived in this region. They just relate to family, to friends and to work, and don't feel comfortable or have any desire to associate with any form of wider community.

That last point is vital for understanding Gerald. He would say it's precisely those who merely exploit the village institutions that tend to see people like himself as driven by the desire to be part of an elite with the power to control. For him, on the other hand, it is all about responsibility. In fact, being a manager means being one of those who serve, one of those who spends all their time working to ensure that all those myriad institutions that constitute the village function and survive to such a degree that they can indeed be taken for granted by those whom he would regard as merely irresponsible or parasitic.

These circles are by no means invariable. In some villages Gerald would seem entirely anachronistic. These are far less hierarchical; in The Glades, people born in social housing can now be found occupying senior roles. The idea of an entitled but responsible elite has faded away. In others, the inner core would still have a masonic lodge and there would be, if anything, more exclusivity and secrecy surrounding their activities than one finds in Gerald's village. Gerald's village has its own particular system and Gerald knows exactly how that system operates. There are several golf clubs in the region but the one that becomes crucial to this particular structure arose because Gerald and half a dozen others from the Lions Club wanted to play golf together and simultaneously joined this particular club which in effect made it the chosen club for the purposes of being able to privately discuss core village matters while at leisure. Gerald also explains how the inner circles control the outer ones. For example the Lion's Club would run the village carnival. As a result, Gerald will himself sometimes help these wider philanthropic and charitable organizations, but he gets impatient with what he sees as their lack of professionalism: 'I am used to working with people who are in charge of major businesses so I can't now sit down with trustees who couldn't make up their mind and chief executives who dither.'

What concerns Gerald is the decline or threat to other core institutionalized positions that have always served as the framework of the village, much as the old oak beams support the most ancient houses. A proper village should have its own post office, its own policeman (what he would call the special constable), a village butcher, ideally also a chemist and a bank. But none of these remain in his own village. The policeman works from the local town, one pub is a restaurant and another is a fast-food outlet. Even those that remain as traditional pubs are no longer run by what Gerald would regard as long-term village publicans with whom you could have a personal relationship and who understand that part of their role is to keep an eye on the more troublesome members of the community. Gerald barely knows who the current publicans are. One of Gerald's key fights is with the church since these days the church simply can't afford to have the kind of village presence memorialized by Trollope. But without their own vicar, Gerald feels the village would no longer have its own church and he wonders aloud whether then it would really be a village. Taking away the vicar would be the final nail in the coffin of a dead village. But things have not yet come to that pass and, for the present, he can proudly affirm that they have still a village cricket team and all eleven players are village lads.

Having established how Gerald sees the village, we can make more sense of his personal life. For him, the family also should and does fall into a similar pattern. The most obvious expression of this is generational. There are quite defined differences between the appropriate relationship with a spouse, then with a child and in turn with a grandchild. His wife has always been true to her role, derived from being the wife of a senior executive. She entirely accepts that her responsibilities lie within her husband's second circle, rather than his inner circle. But she also 'really tends to do the social side of our life. So if we're making arrangements to do anything, because she keeps her diary/calendar more than I do, she is the one who will arrange lunches and visits and that sort of thing.' Because of various company postings abroad, such as Jamaica, his wife's life and work had been pretty disrupted, but they had two daughters and a son, and now have three grandchildren. Initially, the children all went to boarding school.

His own children form a little circle in their own right, each representing a different kind of relationship. At the core is their daughter who lives in the same village. Since he has not been well, she comes to visit them every other day. She is as close a confidant as he possesses, especially in one regard. Gerald knows what is going to happen to him. His anxiety is about what will happen to his wife when he is gone. He can see that her technophobia, which until then he felt was quite becoming to her as his wife, confirming his own comparative mastery of technology, would at his death become quite debilitating, were it not for the wider family. Gerald will engineer for his wife to be absent so that he can discuss these issues with his daughter. The daughter, who was extremely busy at her work but knows full well that he has a particularly aggressive form of cancer, simply gave up her job after learning of his prognosis in order to be on hand for any help that is required. Just as his wife is delegated the family social networking, it is this daughter who Gerald has delegated the responsibility of keeping all three children informed about these conversations.

The next generation is very clearly differentiated. For Gerald, his role is to show continual interest in the activities and achievement of his grandchildren, and for them only to ask tokenistic questions about him, without expecting a response. He is adamant that this should not change because of what is happening to him since that would reverse the proper order of things. 'It's important for you to maintain that. Grandad is interested in grandson. And that's part of being you. You're a grandad, you're nurturing; that's part of the role. And for that to switch . . . it wouldn't fit.' As he also readily admits, 'We haven't modernized our family relationships.'

These gradations are equally clear in his categorization of friendships. First, he considers where these were formed. There are some friends retained from his working life. Then, as with so many people in this study, there are those key friendships that were made during early parenting. The way he starts talking about the use of tokens within babysitting circles flicked a switch in my own memory. I recalled a thesis written at my department of anthropology at University College London. It concerned the formation of money itself – or money-like systems – based not on some ancient society but on the observation of babysitting circles. As Gerald remembered, 'Yes, there was a secretary, who kept the list of pluses and minuses. When you did it, how long you did it for, whether you got double hours for being after midnight. Hugely complicated – you needed a computer to work it all out. You could write a programme and find it was too complex.' As the thesis noted, this babysitting system of tokens soon developed complex issues of debt and gifting, of swapping and barter, storing up tokens against possible future need and then trading them. The anthropologist can observe money-like systems evolving from such practical issues combined with a sense of fairness, planning, reciprocity, debt and investment.

That was probably the time when Gerald and his wife had most friends locally, alongside the later period when their children were involved in many activities from ballet to sports. Once again, we can imagine Gerald operating a kind of social centrifuge that spins everyone out to an appropriate distance. In this case, the innermost circle consists of those with whom they share their Christmas parties, just four or five couples. This is the only group that Gerald would be comfortable to communicate his concerns about the future, or lack of it. Next come the ten to fifteen couples he calls intimate friends that used to be part of their dinner-party circuit. These days, this is less likely to mean actually cooking dinner but rather going out for lunch either to a house or a restaurant. But also, because of their civic responsibilities, these people come together frequently anyway around church or village events, such as the flower festival.

A rather different circle of friends derives from physical proximity, but only very close proximity. 'I'd say people across there we've known for 37 years. Three up the road we've known for

37 years. People on the corner we had lunch with today we've known for 35 years.' It turns out that Gerald knows the people in the nearest eight houses very well, but he barely knows anyone that lives further away than that. The only times this circle expands to the rest of the street are occasions such as the Queen's Jubilee street party.

Overall, Gerald still has a very busy life. On one particular day, he accompanied his wife to a lunch at a charity run by one of the people who lives nearby, talked with some volunteers at a centre for the blind and also had several phone calls, based on emails he had sent the previous day, with friends from the Lions. He also spoke to his cousin's wife in Gibraltar. In the last few days, he had been to church, played golf, seen his daughter and gone shopping in Treeford, as well as honouring his ongoing Lions' communications. All of this is pretty typical – if not the Lions, then it will be the masons; if not that daughter, then maybe a grandchild; if not the blind, then another charity.

Having established these concentric circles of the village, his relatives and his friends, this in turn becomes the best way of understanding his relationship with the media he uses. In fact, what I call 'polymedia', that is, the choices that come to us courtesy of today's proliferation of media, turns out to be one of the most striking expressions of this aesthetic of relationships. Of all the hospice patients, he was one of the most vociferous in his preference for face-to-face communication. At the core of this was his sense of himself as an officer, not a foot soldier, which depends upon a certain kind of immediacy because when you are in charge of a meeting you need to constantly monitor and respond to changing situations. 'And that's the advantage of being face to face; it gives you the opportunity to see the dynamics of the conversation with a group of people. I ran a huge number of meetings because that was part of my job.'

Subsequently everything that happens within the core needs to be face to face – his discussions during golf or about the Lion's Club, but equally those with his wife and nearby daughter. It is their role, in their secondary capacity, to use the phone or emails to take things to the outer levels and then report back to him. With respect to the family, it's an interesting reversal of how things had been for much of his life, when the children were in boarding school and most communication was by letter. Indeed, if there is another form of communication which he felt positive about, it is letters, though he recognizes that letter writing is now a thing of the past.

Stepping out to the next circle, we find the phone, which corresponds directly to the second circle of village organization since this is the medium through which women organize events. Gerald projects this sense of a female humming and buzzing of communication, based on the phone calls and texting that needs to go on in the background. But all of this is secondary to face-to-face communication. He knows that the phone is crucial for his daughter, as well as his wife, since it is by phone that she organizes his hospital and other appointments, and arranges for someone to drive him there and back. She uses the phone to arrange things but not to tell him about those arrangements. His son jokes about Gerald's complete inability to text, despite his considerable technical competence in other areas. Nor can he do voicemail. Given this clear distinction between face-to-face and phone communication, it is not surprising that Gerald dislikes even the idea of webcams which for him represent a messy ambiguity between these two.

The outer circle of Gerald's communication is email. The appropriate use of email is contact with the kind of friends he made when on holiday. Email keeps them in contact two or three times a year, but at a comfortable distance. Typically, these are friends who live in places such as Canada or Australia whom he met on a cruise. Email is on a par with other things he has to do, although with no great enthusiasm, such as getting information about airline tickets or working with committees.

Gerald also expresses his attitude to these devices in the way he uses them. Unlike his subtle understanding of speech, he has a kind of staccato style both in speaking on the phone and sending family-related emails, as though being terse and laconic are ways of keeping these media in their place as mere tools of information. His daughter recalls how he typed about her wedding preparations. His emails were like status updates: 'florist doing such-and-such; mother completed dresses.' He admits his antipathy to phones. 'Yes, I'm very happy to be able to sit by the golf course and say to [his wife] I'm on the way home. I'll be home at 12.15 and we'll have lunch then.' That suits me fine. I spent much of my life in the back of a company car being driven somewhere, with time to think as opposed to answering the telephone. I'm old-fashioned.'

Social media itself is beyond the pale:

and when you go electronically, you go further and further away – it's more dangerous the further away from the person you get, it seems to be. Using Twitter and Facebook, where you present your thoughts to a million friends, not one of whom you know, seems to me to be a much more dangerous exercise than speaking to an individual face to face. The more remote these things get, the less I think they are effective.

His preferences have rubbed off a bit on his daughter. She notes that, compared to most people, she is more inclined to get in the car to go over and talk directly, something she needs to do with her father but has now taken to doing with others as well.

Given the consistency of his views on all that surrounds him, it is no surprise to find that he needs the discussion with his doctor or oncologist to be similarly direct.

And it seems to me it's the same thing that we're doing, in a room just two or three of you, talking about something like cancer. You are trying to read the dynamics of the room, who wants to hear what, and what they mean when they say something – do they really mean what they are saying, or are they passing around something? All of that is face to face, all about the dynamics of a room with people in.

I have a very good relationship with my oncologist, she is absolutely charming. I enjoy – if that's a word – meeting her and talking with her. I feel able to talk freely, and we can laugh and joke, but underneath that we can probe for answers which perhaps I don't want to hear given to me bluntly. And therefore I would not want anything to interfere with the face-to-face aspect.

He gives an example from the previous Christmas when she

knew that the cancer had returned. I knew that – she didn't say, because she wanted me to have a good Christmas. Now, OK, I didn't address the question, I just let it rest in me, that I knew she knew, and she knew I knew, but we weren't going to talk about it. She then called me back immediately after and told me. That to me is what I want because if you send emails, you have either to deny something or to be bold with the truth.

So being direct face to face doesn't mean being blunt or insensitive. On the contrary, he controls meetings through picking up on nuance and is entirely capable of the necessary evasions that prevent open conflict. He is not someone who flinches from fate. He knows what a recurrence of this particular form of cancer means after they had tried chemotherapy, so he has refused further treatment, even though in his case the chemotherapy had been unusually well tolerated and barely affected him. He accepts that he is going to die sooner rather than later. 'And I don't have any embarrassment about talking to people about what my problems are at all. I would prefer to look somebody in the eye and say "I have cancer". There is no point in concealing it.' But then he admits:

You don't actually need someone to say 'I have cancer, and I am going to die from it.' You don't need to go through that conversation. You can personally convey things which people understand without the bold facts being put in front of them. I find that can be done by people talking to each other face to face. It is not as good if you go down the electronic path. Then it becomes more and more difficult to convey things by impression; rather it requires a bold fact, making a statement.

Unlike most of the hospice patients, Gerald is pretty negative about the potential of new media in medical situations. His overriding concern with medical issues is efficiency. 'Being the sort of person I am, once I got into the system I fairly quickly had the operation.' He is very impressed by his local doctor but also by his oncologist; they are both straightforward and efficient. For the same reason, he is really quite resistant to the idea of visiting the hospice, as suggested by Maria, since for him it is a question of simply using the hospice if and when there is a specific purpose. At the time of our conversation, he had never actually stepped inside the hospice. He simply could not see Maria's point about first getting to know the place or having a relationship with it per se. 'I know what service I think you're going to have to provide for me, and you know it doesn't amount to much, pre-thinking about it.' Similarly, he does not want to stray into the terrain of Macmillan or Marie Curie nurses. He prefers to stay within the National Health Service because that way things are clear cut. He doesn't expect privilege, simply efficiency, and interestingly he assumes he is more likely to get this within the NHS than in the private sector, but then the doctors and oncologists he is meeting through the NHS are the kinds of professional people he knows – when they retire, he might see them at the Lions or the masons.

Gerald has a very English relationship with the church. The vicar occupies a position not dissimilar to Gerald's. They are both expected to be present on most of the major committees and village institutions. Gerald has a close relationship with the vicar and, furthermore, he believes in God. Nevertheless, when it comes to things like dying, spirituality and so forth, Gerald states of the vicar, 'He probably knows my state of health, where I stand, and is supportive of me in that way, but he doesn't come here and we don't pray or do anything like that.' Gerald clearly has no desire for his relationship with the vicar to become more spiritual. Praying together smacks of the kind of sentimentality that he has always tried to avoid. He has no desire to embrace such things just because he has cancer. If anything, it is more important for bodies such as the Lion's Club and the masons to know about his illness since it has direct practical implications in terms of finding suitable replacements for the leadership roles he has taken up, not just here but also at a regional level.

Gerald knows there is nothing he can do about the fact that he will die, and die quite soon. But he can do something about the impact of dying. It is important that having cancer should not detract from his sense of responsibility or impinge upon the structure of things. Just because he is dying doesn't mean that he will shift from his clear rule that you consider the welfare of your grandchildren, but you do not mention your own concerns. It doesn't change his relationship with the vicar. He is one of those who rejects the hospice ethos of rethinking the state of being terminal as an opportunity to do something different. By regarding the village only through the lens of practicality and efficiency in the task of self-replacement, he again preserves his responsibility for ensuring continuity in the proper order of things.

It was structure and hierarchy that made him who he has been and, if he does not preserve this during the period of his dying, then what was the point of what he had achieved in life? Eventually, even the solid English oak beams that support the original village homes rot and have to be replaced, but that need not diminish the structures themselves. For Gerald, dying is a final opportunity to confirm, rather than diminish, a lifetime spent bolstering values he has understood and supported from his central position as the maypole.

Story 10

Control Centre

When I explain that I am an anthropologist researching the use of social and other communicative media, it is generally assumed that this means examining the relationship between people and those media. But, hopefully, it is already clear why that makes no sense. These are *social* media. They are invariably used as the means for being in touch with people. We complain that someone is focused on a screen because we can't see who is on that screen. Often that person is being social rather than anti-social; it is just that the person they are with is not the one they are choosing to engage with. Emma, a retired teacher aged 60, shows clearly why we shouldn't even try to separate our relationships with these media from our relationships with people.

Emma simply can't understand the way people talk about these new devices. As far as she is concerned, her iPad is a bloody miracle. Quite amazing. It is as though fate decided to intervene on her behalf. For many patients, a primary concern is to keep control, especially of their relationships. This does not start from their terminal diagnosis; it was always a paramount concern. In *Social Media in an English Village*, I document how people re-purpose Facebook to make it into a device that allows them to keep relationships at just the right position, not too distant but also not too close. They can use Facebook to observe what other people are doing without having to actually interact with them. They thereby turn Facebook into an instrument for preserving, rather than threatening, Englishness.

Having an illness, such as cancer, take over one's own body is bound to be experienced as a loss of control. Equally, chemotherapy, for example, may mean that other people become a threat of infection at a time when one may be weak, vulnerable and emotional. Loss of control may then become a loss to one's self-respect and dignity. Emma appreciates that just at the moment she felt she was losing control over things, a control that she had always thought defined who she was, along comes the iPad which seems to her to give back the very powers she was losing . . . and then some. Her inability to meet people face to face is replaced by a new ability to 'FaceTime' the people with whom she most wants to be in constant contact: her daughter and, above all, her 18-month-old grandson, now living in Qatar since her son-in-law took a job with the airline there.

Initially, she bought the iPad, something she could barely afford, to gain access to photographs of her new grandson. She was also distraught at the idea of missing her grandson's first birthday and equally the first Christmas 'that he knew about'. 'Every week we Skype. She works full time, can't be on the phone every day. You can choose to have a camera on or off, a voice call or video call. Don't want to show my face today, but I think for her, she likes to see me.' Emma doesn't think she could visit; there is no chance of getting travel insurance these days. Skype is especially important since she feels an 18-month-old can recognize her on the screen but wouldn't relate merely to her voice on the phone. In fact, he is starting to get the hang of the thing himself.

He knows how to swipe the pictures; only a year old, but is that good. Also my daughter sends me pictures if I'm not going to see him that week, this weekend, been on the beach, been on a horse, but you know it's nice, pictures, not just conversations. Can email or send direct, my daughter will put, you know, a whole album on.

There are other benefits:

Silly things, like if you watch things at night, watch something on demand. I don't have a TV in the bedroom. If I do have a bad night, I can always find something on there to watch. I just find it great. Matched that with an iPhone; they work together. I found the iPad a real godsend when I was ill. I used it for keeping up with what emails are coming in through work. It did die down quite a lot – from 75 a day, I was getting five a day. I would see something that comes in, need to forward it, but didn't do a great deal. But also things like buying, researching wigs, information about drugs, medical things. I was using my iPad a lot in bed. I did quite a lot of speaking into that, which I thought was great for emails. I've got a friend in Hong Kong. We send each other sort of letters but in email form. Email you use for longer communications. For personal communication I haven't got regular people I email really, except for her.

Subsequently, Emma found that the iPad also suited her issues of control, typical of English people. Emma never goes to the hospice, which for her is represented by one human being only: Justine, the hospice nurse who has taken responsibility for looking after her, constantly monitoring how she is and ready to advise and intervene. Justine is lovely. 'I feel I get on well with Justine. I can talk to her about things I wouldn't want to share with my children or even my partner, to be honest.' But precisely because Justine is becoming a friend, Emma is starting to have the issue typical of English patients with friends and relatives. She feels that has become a 'burden' on Justine, that there must be other patients who need Justine more. Now she wants to take back some control and reduce this relationship to the essential care she feels she really needs.

Emma's viewpoint is crucial for understanding 'Englishness', for appreciating that when people are backing off, it is not necessarily a sign that they are cold or aloof. Emma is not in the least bit unappreciative of the hospice or of Justine. It is the exact opposite. Her relationship with her nurse has become so close that now she is thinking about the needs of the nurse rather than her own. When she says she doesn't want to be a burden, that is exactly what she means and the precise point of her withdrawal.

This is part of the reason she has switched from making phone calls to using email, where everything is coordinated by the same centre of control, her iPad:

Email or text, not phone. Justine was visiting every week at some point, then every other week. Now she's backed off a bit, I know she is there if I've got a problem, email just to update her, don't have to pick up the phone. I know she's busy, so I say, I can just send you an email or text. If I've had a consultation or treatment, I'd update her. I'm pretty sure she is needed. At later stages, people are going to be phoning her and asking her to come. I think it's the same with friends now. We text more than we phone. Email actually takes longer but since I've got that [the iPad], it's a bit easier. I mean, I would text if it was, say 'Can you just confirm what time you said you were coming?' But if I wanted to know about side effects, I would probably prefer to speak about it, or email, so I could put in a little bit more detail, more accurate. Text, for me, is a more immediate and temporary thing. I could text, 'Could you come and supervise me having an injection?

Emma's account illustrates the meaning of this term 'poly-media'. Today we have access to several alternative media, and our choice of which media we decide to use for any particular act of communication has become thereby quite expressive of, among other things, emotional control, asymmetries of power and moral judgements. For example, Emma suggests that men just don't seem to be able to sustain conversations on the phone in the way that women can. Most men make everything short and functional, texts included. So why then does Emma text when she can phone? 'Silly, isn't it? That's what we do now. Don't just go and knock at the door. Don't want to invade their free time. People are busy nowadays, less free time. I'd prefer someone to text me. I'd say I'm out. Which I often am.' She recognizes that most people prefer a medium where each side has control over the timing and the content as compared to the intrusive nature of a phone call. Once it was the net curtain to check if the neighbour was in. Then the consensus was that one should phone first, and not just knock on the door. Now people can text to find out if this is a convenient time to phone, and then phone to find out if this a convenient time to call around. 'It's very non-intrusive, isn't it? People can ask you how you are and you can quite quickly say "rubbish" or "well" or whatever.'

Polymedia become the refinement of social consideration. It's the same with her family:

> If they are working, then I'll try and work out a time that's a good time. Always say, 'Is it a good time to phone?' If they say no, fair enough. People don't say that to me and sometimes I'm wishing they would.
>
> I got diagnosed with cancer last July. I started treatment, really, September. You've got to be well to speak on the phone, don't you? People sent texts when I wasn't well, then text me saying can I come see you when you get better. And I just say no, I'm not up to visitors, sorry. Then they carry on texting me for a bit longer. Because I say to people don't just turn up. Or even phone me. I'll let you know. Sometimes I couldn't phone my mum even. Taught my mum to do texting. I just say I'm OK, but not up to a chat. I used texting as a sort of barrier in a way, a way of letting people know how you were, particularly my mum, but other friends too. But setting up things for when you feel better. I think what's important to me is what the messages said. If I got a text saying 'Heard your news, really sorry', then I wouldn't think much of that, but a lot of the texts didn't say that; they said, 'I'm so sorry, thinking of you. Please let me know if I can help.' It's like having your obituary written before you are dead.
>
> These things tend to be quite involved, don't they? For example, I did have some news about my heart, which is probably OK now. I would probably not want to send something that was half a story. Either you're going to tell somebody the whole thing, or you're not going to. Some things I didn't tell my mum and dad, and I think it's OK now. No, I can't imagine telling people serious news by text. I want to be very careful what I say. When I told my mum, I played it down, but to other people I've told the unadulterated

truth. Like you wouldn't want the doctor to tell you by text, 'I'm afraid its breast cancer', you know. You can't ask questions.

Now I've been in touch with someone who's just starting treatment for breast cancer, just towards the end of what was my worst treatment. I haven't met her, but someone asked me if I could help her in any way. I text her regularly, saying, 'I think you start your chemo again tomorrow, don't you? I hope it goes well.' And I would always do that. Every few days, I would say, 'How are you doing, How are you feeling?' She does find it really helpful. It's not too intrusive, is it? It's not like they have to put an hour aside in case I feel chatty; it's something they can do really quickly, whenever it suits them, and I can pick it up really quickly whenever it suits me. When I wake up, it's still there. I can say I've not had too bad a day today. I don't go back and delete any.

The iPad has helped Emma regain her sense of control in another equally important respect: knowledge. Having worked as a teacher, Emma is used to being the one to give out instructions, the person who is expected to know things. Emma uses her iPad to research her particular cancer, which is not a common one. She thinks she can tell the difference between those websites that weigh up the evidence and those that are merely wishful thinking or anecdotal. This feeling was more pronounced during her period in hospital, which didn't have the same warmth and personal touch as her relationship with Justine. She had felt this was more an act of assertion. The staff there had said, 'Don't look at American websites. Don't believe all you hear on there.' But this is Emma's response:

I feel I'm always better informed because of what I find out. Obviously, he wants to just tell me what's happening, but sometimes I say I've read this or I've seen that. I don't think they like it. I'm not good at remembering exact chemicals but I do get the gist of it. I feel more informed. They don't have as much time to spend with you – ten minutes – even the private consultation sometimes can be brushed away very quickly.

Knowledge gives Emma more of a presence. It gives her weight, makes her less insubstantial, harder to just brush away.

I read support forums but I don't contribute. I'm usually trying to find out something specific, information. If they had a particular side effect. For example, I had severe toothache after a chemo session; turned out to be a problem with my tooth. I knew that, with the chemo, it could affect your nervous system. I was trying to find out if people had had toothache. Actually they did.

I do know someone who's had similar treatment. To stop everyone constantly asking her, she will put online, 'This is where I am today; I had my ovaries out,' you know. That's not me. I can understand if you want to have a more personal, tailored approach. I think I've learnt through this that I am a private person. I wouldn't tell everyone everything. And I don't want to worry people unnecessarily either.

I did quite want to talk to people, but not those who are negative, only those who are going to encourage me, and most people did. If I did feel a bit down some people are very positive and uplifting, I would choose them. Gather strength from other people, being positive about you. Like people saying, 'You look well, you're doing well.' Lady next door had breast cancer five years ago. I like talking to her. There is a lady round the corner. She also had breast cancer. She's been a big support for people who went through it. I don't know if I can talk to people in the same way. I suppose I'm trying to help this person who is going through it after me, but I wouldn't want to go to a group of people who were all worried. I need to take from people a bit, use their enthusiasm to help me a bit.

Cancer has changed Emma's relationship to Facebook because it has changed her relationship to time. Emma knows she has less time in this world, and that time is precious, but, in another way, being ill, she has so much more time. She didn't use Facebook before. She would always say that she simply didn't have the time for such things. But now she appreciates what Facebook does for her. There are her extended family in Sheffield, all those nieces and nephews, the twenty somethings, who put whole albums online. One them just went to Berlin and 'that was nice to see'. Before, she couldn't see why anyone would bother taking a picture of a cake and putting it up on their wall, but now she thinks that's 'a nice-looking cake'. She doesn't put up much herself. Just once, when she went into hospital, she posted a simple message, hoping that the next year would be a good year. She receives encouraging words, but she doesn't really want to post intimate things to such an undiscriminating place. She prefers to take refuge in her iPad and her sense of control. There, on the iPad, she emails her one or two really close friends. On email, 'You can say how you're feeling at the time and they are going to read it, perhaps that day or the next, never know how long it's going to take.' This is the world she controls – keeping people close but not too close.

I would say that mostly I've been very pleasantly surprised by people being very, very kind and supportive and wanting to help as much as possible. I don't think I've had anyone avoid me or anything like that. Though some people, I thought they might have done a bit more, rather than carrying on as if it hasn't happened. I've got a particular friend, who I consider quite a good friend, lives in London, busy single parent. She's one of those people that when we get together, we get on really well, speak all the time, but she didn't increase her contact with me, just stayed at a fairly low level. But most people who I saw like that, every now and then, they increased their contact. Just sending me texts, people telling me they are thinking about me. It's a bit boring lying in bed having chemotherapy for six months. Quite nice getting little texts saying 'How are you?' Bit of entertainment in a way, hearing a little bit about what other people are doing.

Then the useful things – I had an infection and went to stay at •••• for a week. One of my friends brought me in steak and chips from home. When I came home again, she brought me another meal. The friend from Liverpool, who I said I had long conversations with (my husband was in Berlin at the time), she came up to look after me. Anything I've asked anyone to do, everyone says they want to do something, and I try to give people things I think they like doing. And everybody, nearly everybody – I can't think of anyone who hasn't been kind. Maybe not perhaps as available as I thought they would be.

At the same time, Emma wants to meet people, to see old friends and family, because she knows in many cases this will be the last time. Before, there had been only a 25 per cent chance that the cancer would spread. But then it did, and 'I was back with the same oncologist who'd given me this statement. Oh, you know, nothing else to do, can't do anything for you. So yes.' But in tandem with her changed view of time, Emma feels that, in dying, she is also finally living, that before she was 'on a conveyor belt at work, not just at school, spending as much time at home doing things and ticking boxes. I just found it too much; get a life.' Now Emma has a life, but it's a very short one. She can't make appointments: 'I'll never book anything that far ahead because I just don't know now.' Instead, whenever she feels well enough, it is 'just to get out, as you used to. Not even mentioning my illness at all. Totally doesn't need to be touched upon. Getting out and talking, having a laugh. It's just good to have friends. It's essential actually, really is.'

On reflection, the strangest situation was work. There were people Emma had worked with for 30 years at the same primary school, but they never found the right way to communicate. Nothing to do with media; it was more to do with never being sure what was appropriate to that setting. People talked a lot but there were areas they didn't discuss at all. There was a mismatch of intimacy and distance. How was it that, after decades together, things could still be awkward the minute a conversation strayed into more intimate territory? How did those school walls manage to make you feel you had been 'naughty' adults if things ever got too personal? It is the traditional context, not the new polymedia, which explains why there never emerged an agreed, proper, comfortable, way to deal with work colleagues or even some neighbours. Conversation remained superficial. There was no route into depth, no means to slake this thirst for intimacy. Emma is still not sure how to overcome these barriers. And now that she is dying, this really matters because she wants to finally connect with people she has known for 30 years. But, despite all the new media platforms, she still doesn't know how to make relations with her colleagues more meaningful.

However, with her family Emma is now making use of lessons learnt. For instance, before her daughter moved abroad,

Emma used to mind her grandson while her daughter was at work. She could phone her daughter; she could text her. Both were informative; she could discuss things. But after a while Emma realized this was not enough. What her daughter really wanted was pictures of her son, just pictures. Perhaps it was because a picture is so immediate. With pictures, Emma was not a presence coming between them. 'Often I would go there while she went to work. She wanted a picture. It was reassuring for her. She didn't have just to imagine him being happy. If I could find something suitable at the right moment, I would take a picture.' Today, it is Emma herself who feeds off pictures; she devours them. The childminder in Doha has to send photos to Emma, as well as to Emma's daughter. The background is a revelation: the amazing skyscrapers; the endless desert; a visit to a falconry with some of the most beautiful, if rather scary, birds that she has ever seen. Apparently some of them are worth thousands of pounds.

Of course:

The photographs are going to make me more sad as well. Because I can't ... If I haven't seen my grandson in a week, then I get a picture. That's lovely to see, definitely makes my day. I'm not the best at storage. On your phone you just save images, don't you? Supposed to put them in albums; occasionally I do. Share them with friends all the time. If I go anywhere, I'll say that's my grandson. Oh, have you seen ... ? It's about capturing the moment. I love my pictures, I really do.

There is bound to be that sadness; will she ever see her grandson again? Perhaps not, not ever; the last time was the last time. But meanwhile there are those pictures. She seems to treasure these even more than her Skype calls. Skype is a moment, a connection, but a fleeting one, while the picture becomes the treasure, the thing she can store, share, look at again and again. Skype is her grandson at a distance while the photograph can be put in her jacket pocket, next to her heart. It is also the perfected image, her grandson at his smiley best, her angel; even if there are none awaiting her, this angel she has already met.

When she was a teacher, Emma admits she really couldn't understand this desire by parents for an endless stream of photographs of their children while at school in the manner they had come to expect from child carers, even though there was no way a school would permit this. It seemed like an unnecessary nuisance, an indulgence. Why couldn't they just leave their infants in Emma's capable care for a few hours without needing reminders of what their children looked like? Even though she had been a mother herself, Emma hadn't really seen all this in terms of love, the appreciation that you can't 'leave' your child at school. That they are there all the time, in your head, the endless daydreams and the nightmares that something bad has just happened to them, that they are not completely happy, that they might be missing you as you always, always miss them. 'It's interesting. I was cursing at it only a couple of years ago, all these flippin' pictures, but now I have an interest in a person, I'm interested in those pictures, mainly of my grandson.'

As a teacher, Emma is as much an intellectually curious researcher as I am. It is Emma who conceptualizes her iPad as a device that has balanced her loss of possibilities for meeting people with an enhanced new capacity to see people through FaceTime and Skype and especially to overcome the separation represented by Doha. She could mourn her own impending demise, but she also finds it ironic that it is only in the process of dying that she has resolved one of her main conundrums of living: how best to use time. Mostly, though, she neither mourns nor moralizes. She simply finds it interesting and indeed intriguing that she is leaning about these life skills right up until her own death. The conversation is not morbid, but intellectual. It is Emma who does most of the analysis. As so many of these patients found, as long as one is living, one is learning.

Story 11

Our Forum

Emma's story is concerned with using the media to keep in touch with, and control one's relationships to, established friends and relatives. But her iPad also leads to an unprecedented online world of forums and blogs whose contribution also needs to be evaluated. What place do such online relationships have within the offline social lives of these patients? Is this online community similar to, or different from, traditional concepts of community? Hopefully, these issues become clearer through the story of Stephen and Jackie.

Stephen and Jackie have been together for more than 50 years. They met when he was 22 and she was 20. They have lived in the village for more than 40 years. Stephen suffers from a relatively rare condition, primary lateral sclerosis (PLS), and this brings additional problems. It's less likely that there will be specialist nurses available in the region, and it makes it more difficult to develop a support group since patients are too dispersed to attend a local group meeting. As a result, patients may be more dependent on online information, but again this is a problem. Online information about illnesses is pretty haphazard. It is often easy to find six websites that all support the same treatment, which makes this sound authoritative. But some further digging reveals that this is only because they all pinched the discussion from the same single source, which was not especially reliable. Specialist nurses realize that, even if they can't be present locally, one thing that they can do at least is act as mediators for any online group to ensure that everything posted is accurate. But, then, should the patient always see the medical professional as an authority? Jackie notes that:

Medics tend to take it as the truth, but it isn't always the truth. There was actually this consultant who wasn't prepared to listen to what I was saying. Again, you don't expect the GP, don't expect the people you come across, to have heard of it. It's very much a matter of explaining to them that this is not something they need to be ashamed of or to hide – that they have to go into it in the first place. Make it quite clear that this is going to have to be a partnership, not one person in the know and another sniping from the sidelines. That sort of thing. We have trouble with hospitals where they are very unwilling to take that line.

Yes, the hospice has been different. Up until this time last year, we had had very little to do with the hospice at all. Stephen had this thing that if I wanted to go to the allotment I would go, while he could go and come as he pleased. But about July last year another symptom turned up which meant he couldn't actually be left if he was likely to go to sleep. Usually, when you have got someone whose poorly, and they are having a snooze, you can think, 'Right, I can nip off down to the shops.' But now I can't.

He has rapid eye movement sleep disorder. A few years ago there was a husband and wife who loved each other dearly. They went on a caravan holiday and he murdered her. He woke up dreaming there was a burglar and he strangled her. That's an extreme form; others jump out of windows. Things like that. If you wake up out of a nightmare, you can go back to sleep because you know the nightmare won't be waiting for you. But with REM sleep disorder, you remain in that dream and it takes a long time to go away. Stephen fortunately doesn't suffer from burglarphobia, do you? But he will wake up dreaming that he hadn't taken his medication, and the whole next day's dose went down before he was awake. I don't have to wrestle him back into bed or anything, but I do have to say 'Stephen, are you sure you're awake?'

It then became the case that I couldn't leave the house unless someone who can deal with Stephen's social and medical needs can be left in charge. Unless he is able to come with me. The other day we went up to the allotment; I wanted to pick the beans because we might be getting a frost. That was fine, we're able to go. But if I had been wanting you to come in February, it would have been too cold in the car. So at that time I found I was trapped in the house. At that point, the medics down there had a group conference, and Justine and all had a thing, got heads together, made an arrangement. Ended up over the last year with a lot more than we're entitled to at the day hospice in ••••. Have a person come in, reading and things like that, and other support.

Someone came round and said, 'Well, we need to get to know you,' and I do this and that and the other, so that 'before you really need us, we know all about you'. I said I thought that was a bit funny, bit of a waste of time, but now it's come around that we really do need them. And one thing we have found is that anything that the hospice has to deal with is not only good, but it's better than anyone else. I'm amazed at the amount that happens, what's done, the variety of stuff. You don't just go in a taxi and out in a box, which I think is what a lot of people think. I haven't done any courses yet. There's health care, home care. And this is done as a joint venture between the three local hospices. Can have bought-in care. Carer comes in at 9 a.m. on a Friday and goes at 6.30 p.m., and we pay for her. That gives me a day off, time I can look forward to wasting.

Last autumn, when everything was being set up and sorted, this room was hardly ever empty; people coming from this place, that place, some of whom offered help, some didn't. Those were nearly always face to face, after initial contact by phone. They ask if you've got access to the internet. The basic assumption is that if you're over 70 then you haven't, which of course is partly true of some people and not of others. If there was a fire, I would take Stephen, the cats and the computer. Not necessarily in that order because Stephen can sort himself out. So that was visits; they would come and assess. Can't really assess what's in front of you unless you can see it, and people don't always tell the truth. 'Oh, I'm fine,' they say. Or alternatively, 'Oh my God, it's terrible,' when, in actual fact, it's not.

I felt happier with the forum. Had huge numbers of members, considering. We had a few more every week. A lot of them sit and watch, and you know they are sitting and watching. Can you tempt them to come and post? Say they have been watching the forum this past year, can you tell them about this and that? Because Stephen has had the PLS for a very long time compared with most people. You can go down the drain in six months; actually the survival time has been growing. Seven years ago, it was seven years, now it's going into ten, twelve years. The whole thing depends on the date of diagnosis. They start with Parkinson's. Whole trail of going round the various consultants to find out what on earth is wrong. So by the time you're diagnosed, you've had the damn thing for five years. The statistics are totally up the creek. But basically the forum is an exchange of information, of what has worked: 'Why don't you try getting a continuing care package?' That sort of advice, and also explanations. Because Stephen has had it for a long time and because I survive by knowing about things, I have spent a lot of time finding out. So I am used as the simple explanation source. Like, why have they done this, why have they changed my medicine like this? I can tell them, knowing that the moderator will correct it. That's the arrangement we have.

Don't know the number of people who have posted for the last five years. Many are dead; no idea how many at any one time. As time goes on, they form groups, small groups of people. It's a public conversation which everyone else can listen to. And it will be, you know, did you enjoy your holiday? Did you manage to get an insurance company? That sort of thing. And when she comes back, she will say, 'Oh, how is everybody? I've been watching. You're OK? Sorry that so-and-so had an infection' – very personal things like that. No photos. I don't know whether there could be, whether it could be done, but probably better if it isn't. You're judging people purely on their words and actions, not on what they look like. I look at it every day, twice sometimes.

There's a youngish man in Belgium. He had to give up work. Couldn't find a forum in Belgium. He came and joined us for a time: 'If I give up work, will that stop me having a get-up-and-go attitude?' But I get a lot in the giving. If I go on and say Stephen has been poorly, I'll get suggestions, and they'll say they're thinking of me. I think it's very important. I would miss that dreadfully. Young people are coming in and doing it now, changed the feel of it, different things, new things, setting up local hubs, things like that.

You have to be careful with forums. In general, you get a lot of very bad information. 'My auntie took an aspirin and died' – that sort of thing. I do try to be careful. Unless people choose to give their emails, we don't even know where they live. PLS Trust has a system whereby you can ask to be an email buddy or telephone buddy, can mix, can be one to one or two to two. They match people through head office, have the information on people who want to be matched, who have opted to do it this way. I mean, after a time, you get a pretty good idea where a lot of them go. They tell you they've gone to Stockport hospital, or other people say they live in the lakes. But, no, you haven't got time to go chasing around and seeing people. And most people haven't got time to take guests in.

Where we used to live before, there were five houses in a close. But because it was such a close close, if you know what I mean, the houses were close together, no one wanted to live in each other's pockets, and nobody wanted to share. People at number one, they were the people that drove me out in the end because they were so nosy. And they sat behind their shutters, their blinds whatever, watching. They were obviously watching you. And I found it more and more disconcerting, the worse it got. Go to the back door, key in the back door, and I knew I was being watched. And I could feel these eyes watching me. And several times I'd turn my head, and there they were, the pair of them, just watching. It was horrible. And in the end, I thought, I cannot stand this any more. Never talked to us. All they wanted was information. They'd come over and say where did you get that from? Who's your builder? Who's your electrician? Feeding them info all the time. And I thought, Go away, leave me alone. And every time you looked over, you'd see one or other or both of them at the windows watching you.

But where we live now, we know a lot of people, all very good neighbours, some of them very helpful. Our next-door neighbours that way are very helpful. It's a two-way thing; I mind their chickens, they mind the cat; that sort of thing. One of those families that's always on the go but occasionally if an ambulance turns up to deal with Stephen, because he's fallen, she's always round immediately. Hasn't got time to do a lot of helping, but I can always rely on her for transport. Takes the baby with her. Over the road, the people have only been there a short time and we don't know who they are. On the other side, one couple who've lived here as long as we have. It doesn't work as a community; everyone is so busy. This is the great thing, but if ever we needed any assistance we'd have half a dozen doors to knock on, no problem. Man over the road, he comes and helps and says if you want Stephen sat with, we'll do it. They're all extremely busy. Next door but one, she's just taken a degree in international aid, moved in when we did. They are busy.

The last time I actually asked for help was three years ago, when Stephen had a road accident. I had an operation two days before and I couldn't drive. We had a driving rota. They would take me in and someone else would collect me and bring me back. Our other contacts are people from our political life because we did a lot. The thing about politics, if you join a political party you tend to do it for a reason, which means that other people who think that's a good reason will join it about the same time. There was a big intake of people who joined it when we did, who tend to be ten years older than us. Instead of mid-70s like us, they're in their mid-80s; about four of them have died.

I was a councillor, as was Stephen. A week is a long time in politics. We are Labour and now this area is true blue. And the four political parties I think are finding terrible trouble to get younger people. They are out at work till 8 p.m. at night, get home shattered. If you get a younger person, you grab onto them. Older people can't drive. We used to do a thing at the Rotary fete each year, used to do something with cakes. Gradually, as people have got older and moved away, we have been left with a core of three, who brought a cake, a couple of cakes, over the last three years. Now one has died and another has become ill; that's the way things go. Still, some people there are still friends. Susan and Shirley come and sit with you and read to you, talk politics.'

Story 12

Depression

One of the most surprising findings of a research project about hospice patients was the almost complete absence of any expression of anger or resentment that might be expected to follow a terminal diagnosis. Even with Juliette, a business woman in her forties, it felt more like sullen resentment, and the cause was not so much impending death but the sense that right from the start it was life that had betrayed Juliette. The result was not anger but rather depression.

Things had been difficult for Juliette right from her schooldays when she was bullied, partly because she stood out as a redhead and partly because her mother taught at the school. Perhaps the fact that she played the banjo didn't help. Other girls would regularly take away her pen or books so she couldn't work 'but the teachers wouldn't do anything about it because they'd turn around and say stop telling lies. So, you're stuffed.' A key problem had been the school's ethos, at that time a very liberal outlook opposed to things such as discipline and hierarchy. But this resulted in a lack of control, a refusal to curb those children who took advantage by bullying others and yet were regarded by teachers as simply expressing themselves.

Worse still, her parents were at the extreme end of this liberal anti-authority stance, to the extent that everyone else dismissed them as anachronistic hippies. She was banned from playing any sports that could be construed as competitive. Her parents were seen as the sort of people you expect to see in Amsterdam but not in the vicinity of this village. She had no friends; she was just a weirdo, easy to pick on. Even today, she can't escape her loathing of her school. Recently, 'I couldn't go into the buildings without getting a cold sweat, from what I experienced as a kid. Couldn't do it.'

After finishing her schooling, she set up a business. However, such liberal schools were 'arty', and she developed a complicated but original process for creating a form of ornament that worked well as a gift. It was a real struggle, but at least it was starting to get somewhere. She was getting orders from London firms that suggested this might well become an established enterprise. But then some kids from a local 'problem' family burnt her workshop down. In fact, they did this twice. The first time it was a small fire. 'And they said "Don't worry, they won't come back." Two weeks later, fire engines everywhere, the whole friggin' thing goes up.' Even with compensation, a business that cannot be relied upon is no business at all. Finally, the local council moved the family out, and since then there has been no trouble, but the damage was done. But then at far too young an age she was diagnosed with some illnesses that caused her a good deal of pain over several years. And just as there was some hope of relief, along came this cancer, not just cancer, but what she regarded as the worst cancer there is. She should know; her cousin died of the same thing.

If you are already not that experienced or successful at making friends, cancer really doesn't help much.

I don't feel unwell, but apparently I am. People's reaction to you changes. They don't know what to say. There was a time when my mother was having coffee mornings, inviting my friends round and telling them all about my cancer. I stopped her doing it because all of a sudden people wouldn't talk to me. So there's a lot of inappropriate behaviour around this stuff.

Once again, she feels her parent's liberalism, their well-meaning openness, has come back to bite her. She tries to explain to them that it's her illness, her responsibility. It should be up to her to tell people or not to tell people, to judge where it is appropriate and where it is inappropriate to talk about these things; because for some people it simply isn't. 'If you go out there and tell the neighbours, they'll just stop talking to me . . . They treat you differently, they avoid you.'

It's the same when her mother goes through Juliette's dustbins, just in case there is something potentially recyclable that Juliette had failed to spot. It was just about all right when she did this before, if vaguely irritating, but when she has cancer this really does makes her angry.

She'll empty it all out, and she'll go through it. And I said it makes me feel really bad inside. I want to feel that feeling of actually throwing it away and it's gone. I don't give a toss whether it's recycled or not. It's gone, out of my life. And then I find the stuff back in all different places. I don't want that feeling. But she doesn't understand it.

Recycling is much more important to her mother than having a psychologically clean environment. 'My psychological needs at the moment for some reason have been heightened. I'm very sensitive to it.' Juliette really needs to get rid of these childhood torments, but her family just don't get this at all. They think there is some green, ecological ethos that will make her feel better about death. Some humanistic sense that her elements will re-join the universe and provide some sense of immortality, all atoms together again. At these times, she wishes they would 'just fuck off'.

Juliette has noticed that there is one thing that really does seem to make a difference.

> People can't connect with cancer, or connect with illness, unless they have first-hand experience. They can't orientate themselves around it, so they back off. In your life, you only need to know about six or seven people. That's all you need, really. It's a few people that make the difference. The rest are really irrelevant. If you look back on different pasts and what made a difference, the number of people is very few and far between. The rest of it is just, really, not important. You're spreading your time and resources so thinly. I much prefer to have a half-hour conversation with someone that's really deep, really gets somewhere, than have just flim flam. I've now stopped communicating with the family because you don't know where it's going.

At first, when she was given a terminal diagnosis, knowing that there would not be that many conversations left, it became important to Juliette that these should have quality. She can't stand the idea that she is speaking on the phone and then realizes the other person is driving at the same time. Face to face is not enough in itself. It's all about whether they are paying attention, giving themselves completely to that conversation. She doesn't want to just have a drink with someone. She knows that while dying, she is casting around for evidence that life itself has some significance, some depth, some authenticity. But when that never really developed the way she had hoped, when it became clear that there was no new depth or profundity from knowing that she was dying, she went instead into a kind of retreat. 'When I was diagnosed, they basically said go home and die, there's nothing else we can do. I said OK, so I'm treating myself. And I have been since January last year.' Juliette's main response was the decision to up sticks and move to a really remote rural location.

When I first got here, I was only able to walk about a little bit. I had just moved into a lovely place in the countryside. I just smiled and said this is heaven. I thought this is what I needed, after all the stress and grief I got from my previous life. So I was ready. I was exhausted. I wasn't very well. So it was heavenly to be here; could be out and wouldn't bump into a soul. And then when I did bump into people, they were so lovely. Other places, there's morning and peak times. Wouldn't even know it was peak time here. No rush-hour traffic. And I think that's how I am quite lucky. Just horses now.

The neighbours I've got to speak to, they say you could be here 30 years before you become a local, but I've mixed in, which is lovely. I do know a couple of neighbours. One, his wife has cancer as well. There is also a retired Macmillan nurse, although I've never seen hide nor hair of him. I was saying to you earlier that when I was first diagnosed everyone was contacting me. Now, nothing for months. Nothing. No one does anything. No one checks how are you doing, nothing. And I heard much the same from other cancer patients before I finished my treatment. You know, you're swamped when you are having your chemotherapy, with everyone. Then you stop your treatment and – *boosh* – no one wants to know. It's so true. So true. Very strange.

With regard to communication, I find myself now, more and more, that I just don't want to bother. I've been like that since chemotherapy and I've just got worse. I just don't want to. Sometimes I let it go to answer machine if it rings; can ring them later. I'm not bothered. I'm quite happy to not have any communication with anyone. I don't even email, don't bother. I've kind of withdrawn completely. I'm not on social media. I would never contemplate signing up for Facebook. I would never. When I used to go to work, I used to spend all day on computers and it's the last thing you want to do when you get home. I find it remarkable how much time people spend on computers. I don't understand why people tweet how they are feeling. I think that Facebook can be a real downer actually: the deaths, people my age. And just people's moods and, I don't know ... Watching the news this evening, actually it's the same old, same old, and you see the same pressures. Yet they are still going on about it, not solving anything.

I know it's ideal, a lot of communication, but I think it's a bit too much what you find out when you're not really prepared for it yourself. I can't deal with it, especially when I have the cancer. Just seem to find out how many other people have cancer, so it wasn't always good. I have not found anything positive either. The amount of info you get given from the cancer unit and from everyone else. Too many mixed things from different people. You've got the Macmillan, the Cancer Research.

I think the world has become an explosive place. That's how I feel personally and I've felt that for a long time. But I feel now that I don't want to be part of it. I don't want to be stressed. Think I'm quite strict now because stress isn't good for the cancer. I know how much stress I was having prior to being diagnosed, and I'm refusing to allow that to happen again. But if you're out in the real world, or watching, it's stress. But I'm not one to just close my eyes. I want to do something. I think that's part of the problem at the moment, that I don't know what to do, don't know who I am. I think that that's maybe why I need to be on an island on my own, to understand myself.

The hospice ring me every couple of weeks and I go up once a fortnight for treatment. They're lovely. They are godsends, they really are. Since they've taken me under their wing, I don't feel alone any more. I've got a nurse, counsellors. And they are all so wonderful, love •••• on reception. I could have done with them a little bit earlier while I was actually going through chemotherapy.

I don't have the physical energy to do things. I have a pile of papers and I could just shut myself in a cupboard and not deal with it, not respond to anything. And that's so not me. When I was working, I was so organized. Everyone would come to me because I was so good, and I loved my work. But not any more. I just feel that I'm swamped by everything. I'd love a holiday. I haven't had a holiday in ten years. I needed a holiday before all of this so I really could do with a holiday now. Just to be isolated. I would love to have nothing, just nothing.

I'd like to be more isolated. I'm quite happy with that. I have been depressed over the last few months. That's something I've suffered, along with my health, suffered a lot of pain throughout the years. And while I've been very depressed – this sounds really terrible – part of me would say that I'm quite angry that I've been given this second chance of living. I really would be quite happy to end my life. That's not me saying I would do anything because I wouldn't. I've been down that route a few years ago. It's not dragging me down. That's how I feel. I'm just angry that I'm feeling that way and that maybe I've got that second chance. I don't know.

With the hospice, if the phone rings, I think, 'Oh God, who's that?' That's how I am. It's my choice; it's helping me. Having some therapy has been really good. I probably should have spent more time there to sit in the peace and quiet. There's nothing that's going to give me stress there. No one is going to make me do anything I don't want to do. It is just that, for me, I don't know what's coming next. Although I don't think anything else could shock me any more, I can sit and smile, but when you're gone, I don't feel like that. Not feeling miserable, but I don't have to put the smile on. Some days, I mean, don't get me wrong, days when I'm not well, I am in a lot of pain and just feel out of sorts and I can't – just can't – face anyone or anything. Because when I'm like that. I don't particularly want people to see my suffering. Does that make sense? I just plod on and when I can't, I can't. But I don't want anyone else. I think too many people have seen that pain over the years.

I haven't even contacted my best friend, nor my sister. Not in touch with them now, haven't spoken to them for months. I guess if they phoned I would take the call. Sometimes I don't want to. I don't know . . . you know what I think it is. I haven't breathed, I haven't had breathing space since the second I got diagnosed with that illness and then the cancer, then going through chemotherapy. I haven't breathed. I haven't. I don't feel that I have. I feel that I want to be on my own somewhere, on my own, no phones, no TV, nothing. Just for me to stop. That's what I'd like. If I could live on an island with no one, I'd be very happy right now.

Story 13

Community

Having decided to work in rural villages, I was surprised how long it took to form any clear idea as to the role of community. 'Maypole' figures, such as Gerald, are now quite rare. But I had certainly expected to meet far more people like Elizabeth and Richard, now retired and in their sixties. It was almost a relief when we finally did meet them.

Elizabeth would rather talk about the hospice in terms of what she does to help them, rather than the help she received as a cancer patient. This was not uncommon. The hospice has had a huge impact locally, quite apart from caring for terminal patients. Practically every village over a certain size, and certainly every local town, has a hospice shop. These have come to dominate the charity shop sector, itself a significant presence in the high streets of Great Britain. They are typically staffed by volunteers and have become a key point of socialization mainly for retired women in their locality. People within the ethnography that I was simultaneously carrying out in the village talked about their specific role within the shop, discussing who had just helped take the money and who had a more managerial position. In effect, they often had hospice shop friends who they met frequently, depending upon the rota for volunteers at that particular shop. But, as is already clear from other stories, friendships within the public domain are quite separate from private friendship. This is not to belittle the impact. Hospice shop friends were often quite significant in people's lives. As exemplified by Elizabeth, one could also simultaneously be both a hospice patient and a volunteer at a hospice shop. But that was merely one of a litany of voluntary activities that Elizabeth had been involved in.

I have been doing neighbourhood watch for 35 years. Still active. Well, I've actually delegated the bulletin now to my friend who lives in Park Road. But I think about two thousand houses get our bulletin. I used to have all the Neighbourhood Watch meetings here. I'm sure it helps that crime is low. We're not as involved with the road as we were previously. People know to look out for each other, you know. Well, for example, if a neighbour leaves their car lights on, someone will obviously go and tell them. In our road, I organized street parties for twenty-odd years. I did it with a friend at the top of the road and we passed it on to young mums saying we've done our bit, you do it. So it's all so sad. I think it's like a lot of things, the young come in, but they're too busy to do other things, so busy. I might be wrong but I don't think the next generation is as community minded as my generation, our generation.

When I was first diagnosed, I told my mum and my younger brother face to face, and then my mum told my other brother, and my brother told my dad. My mum told my auntie and she told my cousins. But then subsequently with my cousins, I Facebook with them a bit. And then my dad would have told my aunties on that side. I didn't do a lot of face to face. Everybody else did it for me. Some people that I wouldn't have seen, I emailed or texted.

I'd never have phoned everybody; it would have taken too long. People are very different about this. Some who have a cancer diagnosis never tell very many people. But I thought because I come across so many people in my day-to-day life, I don't want to hide things. I'm going to tell everyone straight up from the beginning. I'm talking about quite a lot of people. Probably about fifty that I keep informed: my mum, dad, two brothers and my sister in Australia, auntie, cousins. I did a lot of community work which isn't paid. At the time of diagnosis, I probably would have most of those people on my email. There were also maybe a dozen people in my work group.

I had a round-robin email. In the initial stages, whenever I had a treatment – tests or something – maybe I would send about four of those. The first one wasn't brief but the others were. Quite a few of those emails were not sent by me but by my partner. A lot of the time, when you are first diagnosed, you're actually really busy. There's a lot of appointments. You're in the hospital. I had my operation, in hospital for a week. There were updates and things going on then, but I wasn't part of any of that. Had tons and tons of texts from people. Or they would find out from a friend, would meet someone in town, say have you heard about •••• and would text me.

I would never have posted on Facebook. I have become quite old fashioned about this privacy thing. I get quite nervous about putting stuff like that out on social media. I can't quite get to the bottom of it but I can't put anything on social media that's anything to do with me personally. I think texts are a very positive thing. I made a point of making sure I keep them because they are a little bit like in the past when you'd get cards. I did have a load of cards as well. Nice to know people think of you, want to help if they can. Downside, of course, is that unless they say 'Please don't bother replying to this', then you've got an implied need to reply. You can back them up, in the ether. I found it was quite helpful to remind myself of the timeline of what happened. I haven't kept a diary or anything. But looking back on those texts, I can see I was diagnosed on this day and then this series of events happened. I could follow that through the text trail. Like a memory. Nice to go back every now and then and read nice things. Same reason I kept all the cards I got; every now and then I have a quick shifty through them.

Had quite a lot of visits where people dropped off presents for me and stayed for a cup of tea. Overall that was nice. I had some visits when I came out of hospital. I did go through a phase – I think it was when I came out of hospital and before I started my chemo. I had some old friends who wanted to come and visit. I really didn't want anyone to come. I kept putting people off. I know there have been times during the years I was diagnosed where I've had more energy and have been much more up for social interaction or face to face, and other times when I haven't. I guess it's important to recognize that, as people go through treatment and the illness gets worse, they may well change their preferences.

When I was first diagnosed, I felt that the amount of people who communicated with me was right for that time in that I didn't feel overwhelmed by it, and I didn't feel that I needed to look for more people. And then there have been other times during the whole year where I have wanted to expand that network because I felt a different need. For instance, one of those needs is talking to people who've had breast cancer because people who haven't had it don't understand some aspects of it. And I guess the other thing I've noticed is that, say in a group of a hundred people that you know, who know about your illness, certain people sort of float to the top and become people that are really there and do things for you, and really help. And it's quite interesting that those people are not always the people that are your closest friends or that you would expect. For us, it was particularly noticeable when I was in hospital. People would just turn up and leave a stew on the doorstep, and they were people that were friends, but not those I would necessarily count as my closest. I do wonder if what was different was that those people may possibly have had experience themselves of what it's like to go through that kind of experience, whether it be themselves or their family.

The neighbours are quite good. A lot of them are older. Sadly, one neighbour, she's only in her early fifties, is getting the results today of a not-very-good mammogram. Her mum had a full mastectomy. So tonight at 5 p.m. she's going to learn. And I know how I felt when I was told – that waiting time after you've had the biopsy and they think there is something wrong and you've got five or six days to wait before you know. So when we were told this the day before yesterday, I just texted her and said I'm so sorry: if you want to talk, you know I'm here. Something like that. She appeared at my door and she did talk and say how frightened she was, and I said in one way this is the worst time. But once you know, either you are going to be really joyful or you can think right now I've got to fight this. So I'm just keeping my fingers crossed for her.

My neighbour's very helpful. But it's not necessarily people from the same street but from the village. I would say that at least half of the people we know here must have offered some kind of practical help at some point. I feel like I'm part of a very strong connected thriving network. And I know all my neighbours. A lot of my transition town [a transition town is a movement to create local self-sufficiency] friends were very supportive. We do quite a lot, but one of the things we are grappling with is that people don't know who we are, though we are connected to bits of the community. So the hospice director ran a couple of sessions called 'building community days', where we invited different community groups about the town to see how we can come together. A lot of my time is taken up doing work related to that. Rather tangential.

The other thing I've been quite involved in locally is issues around school provision and school-based planning. When we first arrived here, I had a problem getting my son into the school and there was a big issue about it. I ran a big campaign. I was quite instrumental in that, got it fixed and sorted. And my network expanded hugely within the space of about a month. I must have met 300 parents in the town over a short period of time. So in a sense that investment was paid off by the fact that I had a very good network of people who came when I needed the help. The same with the transition town thing. The same with the neighbours. It's karma in that way.

By contrast, Richard recalls how his main contact with other villagers originally came through his football and cricket coaching. He experienced some of the 'class'-based tension between the two sports. He saw how the cricket team had to gradually recognize that the 'rougher kids' who played football were actually needed if the cricket team was to maintain its quality.

I suppose if you look at the village, the cricketers have got their pavilion and their bar and everything, but football hasn't got that. They may use the changing rooms, but the bar and stuff is still part of the cricket. There's always a bit of friction. I think that, with the village activities, it's not so much the actual sport. It's the social side afterwards that is more important, especially locally.

The problem is that as he has got older, sport no longer really worked in terms of active community involvement. So it was really through Elizabeth becoming unwell that a whole new dimension of involvement also opened up for Richard.

Richard: So then I started working with volunteers who support the hospice, doing some driving. There are the meetings which are part training, part finding out what's happening, part update. And then there is the person who has identified a carer who needs support, and who then identifies the best person to give that support, who will then phone. And then we'll arrange to meet. Immediately after any visit, I will phone to say everything is all right. One of the problems is that my hospice liaison person, like a lot of people, is not a full-time employee. I think she probably has a terrible time divorcing herself from work, especially because of these phone calls all the time.

So then she introduces me to a carer. We independently arrange when I'm going to go. Typically, it is Tuesday 10 a.m. (or whatever). There are lots of different types of volunteers here. I receive quite a few phone calls unrelated to my role. But they keep one up-to-date with what's happening in the hospice. My point of contact is Justine. I let her know if there is a problem. For example, I went to one person and couldn't get an answer. Then discovered that was because he'd been taken into the hospital for a few days. But it hadn't got back to Justine. So that just exposed a slight flaw here in the communication, but she is aware of that flaw. She is chasing it up.

My job is to give carers some time off by sitting with their patients. An hour, two hours, probably on a weekly basis. Some of the others in our group have people they've been visiting for a year or two; really a very close relationship. It is set up on a regular basis: it could be once every fortnight, once a week, and has a degree of predictability to it. I don't think there is anything which says you can't have more than one.

My other connections with the hospice are also through driving. There's a pilgrim group once a month and there's a lady who I used to bring here for regular meetings. She had just recently been bereaved so she came for counselling, but now she's stopped attending the group. And that was quite an interesting one because she said she found the chats that we had in the car very useful. I gave her a little bit of my philosophy about getting out there because nobody is going to come to you. So she joined the University of the Third Age, went to a choir, went on holidays, tried internet dating and things like that. She said some of that was as a result of the conversations she'd had with me.

Right at the beginning, I was a little hesitant because I wondered if I should be talking or not, wary that what I might say might contradict what others might say from a counselling or therapy point of view. Every month, she always had a bottle of wine there for me as a 'thank you' and now she's working at the charity shop in •••• on a Wednesday afternoon. So, yes, I think we did get on very well. She's doing well.

All of the people I drive are in the upper age group, such as a lady in her late eighties who could actually have driven herself but during the winter didn't believe she could. Another lady – you learn so much from these people – this one said she came along because she found it devastating when her sister had died. Husband not a problem, but sister really hit her. Sister lived very close to her. They obviously had a very close relationship. I enjoy doing the driving, I have to say.

Elizabeth: It's interesting when people talk about community. In my experience, community is very strong, but something we are very aware of in the transition town movement is that we don't know who the people are that we are connecting with. It is difficult connecting with hard-to-reach groups or to get elderly men involved unless they are a certain type that are going to join the Rotary. Or you see certain families who maybe have their own very close friendship network but don't engage in any wider community stuff.

I'm on a HOPE course and six other people on the course have shared that their family have left them isolated, that friends have disappeared. And I think, 'How does that happen?' And every week I'm so grateful for not having had that experience. The question is how do you get to those people early enough so that the hospice can be effective and change their experience of both their illness and potentially their death? Sometimes the hospice has got to go to the community, rather than people going to the hospice.

I don't think people are coming in so much now because of my condition. I think it makes people nervous. One came around but it wasn't really to visit me; it was to ask Richard a favour. She brought me flowers.

Richard: They don't phone because they're not sure how they're going to find Elizabeth. I said she's OK to talk.

Elizabeth: I'm very hurt that we haven't seen our best friends since I was diagnosed. And they hardly phone. And I find that very upsetting that, you know, that they can't even find time to pick up the phone. Richard actually saw Joan on the bus on Saturday. And I'd phoned her six weeks earlier. And she said,

'Oh, I'll be in contact next week and we'll come up for a cuppa, or even come down to us.' Nothing. And then she actually saw Richard on the bus.

Richard: We've always said to phone if they want to come and see us. Either she's fine or, no, she isn't. Much easier. But they don't. I suppose they didn't know how emotional we were going to be. You couldn't have anyone come in then because we were just going to pieces in the early days. We were told on the Thursday and I think we went to pieces all over the weekend. And then I got up on Monday morning and thought this is ridiculous. Got to face up to it, be positive. And you know, we got better after that. We just decided that it's silly being morbid and looking on the black side. Got to look on the positive side. It's a bit like a bereavement. You're so worried about saying the wrong thing that you don't say anything at all. Yet if you meet someone in the village, it's OK. Outside the home. They see you out and think, 'Oh, you must be feeling better.'

Elizabeth: We've told you about friends who haven't come up. But I've got another friend who lives at the other end of Bishop's Avenue. She phones me every week without fail. Today, I phoned her – said I beat you, I've phoned you, and she apologized for not phoning me. And I said, 'Don't be daft.' And we're going to go round for a cup of tea, not next week but the week after. We had actually made previous arrangements to go for a cuppa with them but I was going through a bad time so we cancelled. We went to a funeral on Wednesday and it was very touching, wasn't it? Because at the church they were saying prayers for me. Very touching how quite a few people came up to talk to me. The doctor, people I have known through

Neighbourhood Watch again. We bumped into the warden in Waitrose last week and, you know, she was so lovely. We're saying our prayers for you, and I said I know, that's so lovely. I was at the hairdressers – you know, the one next to the post office. I was nearest the window and the poor girl couldn't cut my hair because everyone was coming in to talk to me. The local police assistant came in. Five or six different people came in, which was so touching, so lovely. I was very humbled by that.

Story 14

Bluebells

The landscape surrounding this largely rural area is beautiful in a particularly English way. It is gentle and modest. There are no mountains or even hills, but the fields and paths have slopes and ridges, so views gradually emerge and fade as though not presuming to occupy too much of your time, just enough for you to appreciate the offerings of that season. Even the most remarkable of these presentations, the annual show of bluebells, creates a haze of colour that cascades down a wooded enclave such that no individual bulb gets to show off. After a while it seems entirely appropriate that Bernard and Jeanette should have chosen this little cul-de-sac of sweet-looking but unpretentious homes that fit precisely the character of their occupants.

As so often with hospice patients, they will start apologetically, convinced that they could not possibly be of any interest to a research project. There must have been some mistake that led us to them in particular as against all the really interesting people we could have been spending our time with. But they had agreed for us to come and now that we are here, of course, they are happy to help. What Bernard and Jeanette will assist us in understanding are two important general points. The first was that it could be older rather than just younger people who seized the potential of new media, and, secondly, this is a story that starts to hint at some of the problems that arise from this characteristic English modesty.

At first, the only background to discussing media use is that Jeanette spent her life working as a teacher and Bernard as an engineer. It must have been at least an hour before we ascertain that she has written a book and that he is a master craftsman in the creation of clarinets. Certainly, she had been a teacher, but there was so much more. She has also been involved in a huge range of educational activities including organizing the school governors, pastoral care and national examinations. She had held several quite senior positions while also looking after their several children. It was that experience that led to her collaboration in writing a book about these wider aspects of working in schools. There were plenty available about teaching, but a neglect of the many other duties and possibilities that almost invariably form part of the wider engagement with education as a profession.

For Bernard, life hadn't really expanded within the compass of his formal job, which remained limited, and he had taken early retirement as soon as he could. Instead, he had developed himself through his devotion to classical music. Together, they had created the ideal place for this late flourishing. The house lent itself to home making with its flint walls, alcoves in the corner and hand-made bricks and tiles. But they had gradually added the ornamentation that gave it such character. A stranger coming in didn't know the personal stories that linked each ornament to the couple, but immediately sensed that everything had its story, and that they too would feel cosy and coddled; 'friends that we have to stay, they think it's like a convalescent home, love coming because of that. Even our son says it's so relaxing.'

As two 80-year-olds, they could easily have impressed us with the range, originality and effectiveness of their knowledge and usage of new media. But they talked as though the opposite was true, that they were technophobic, excusing their use of the media by explaining that it was only the pressure from their teenage grandchildren that had foisted these icons of modern life upon them, and that they were probably using them all in the wrong way or at only a fraction of their potential.

Certainly, the younger generation had helped, sometimes the youngest. Jeanette's grandson had been devoted to computing since he was six, building his own website by the age of nine. Bernard remembers the early conversations. '"Well, Grandad, click on the icon in the bottom left-hand corner," and I'd say, "There isn't one," and he would say, "There must be, Grandad." And then he'd say, "Oh. Oh, well, we'll have to do it another way, then."' Actually, Jeanette's own disabilities also played a part. She has had increasing difficulties with her hearing to the point that she actually rather dislikes the phone now and distrusts her ability to use it properly. Also, phone calls bring back bad memories for her of the hour-long phone calls she had been expected to make every week to her own mother. These had tended to be bad-tempered and awkward, and she had always been glad to get them over with. Phone calls come at inconvenient times and one is not prepared for them. This experience had first encouraged her to use emails, over which she feels she has far more control. It also dispels the anxiety she experiences on the phone that she will be too soft-spoken for someone to hear, but it seems rude to ask them to shout. However, she recognizes that, with email, 'other people will read into it things you don't intend. Might get upset by something you said that you didn't intend at all. Got to be very careful with your choice of language.' For her, email is also the medium through which she sends, receives and shares photographs. Later, this encouraged her to use a webcam since it is important for her to see the person while they are speaking.

Today, it is Bernard and Jeanette who feel upset that their contemporaries simply won't have anything to do with new technologies. They all seem just too concerned that they might make a mistake, might damage something. By contrast, Bernard and Jeanette follow the pattern of younger people in that they now sort their friends by media preference. They have an email friend in Cornwall, and a phone friend in Nottingham. They have learnt that it's often easier to align oneself with the 'comfort medium' of another individual. In their eighties and with six hip operations between them, they are acutely aware that it is people of their age who most need these new communications. This is especially so during post-operative periods of immobility, when living in an isolated rural environment can become a problem. As they admit: 'People don't know their neighbours round here. The front doors, you go into your property and that's it, close your door . . . not that we wouldn't be welcome. Just norm.' It is outsiders who are summoned to help when they are ill. They would simply never ask a neighbour for help; it's too intrusive: 'I take pride in that, actually, in being private with those sort of personal things. People have their own problems; don't want to take on board other people's.'

It was a granddaughter who helped Jeanette see beyond the idea that modern media is somehow opposed to their own sense of craft. They were very impressed when she taught herself to knit simply by watching YouTube videos, after which 'she started a knitting club in the class and enrolled the boys. She always says, "Oh, Grandma, can you knit, can you crochet? Look what I've made for my teddy."' Jeanette taught her how to quilt, but at the same time she would teach Jeanette how to text. So after a while they could see using media as something alongside craft, perhaps even a craft in its own right.

For Bernard, too, there was a natural fusion between traditional craft and new digital capacities. Increasingly in his retirement, he has devoted himself to the repair and making of clarinets. He used to play in an orchestra where he helped people by repairing their instruments. He started making his own around twenty years ago, with the metal parts sourced from Germany. But he knows that today his independence, his ability to live where he has settled, is mainly thanks to Amazon.

Amazon is the foundation for what he can make. But, for the consumption of music, another site has come to the rescue. Bernard just can't believe how useful Spotify can be:

I read something in the paper about a musician or something, then I go onto Spotify. Every night I use it. I think it's absolutely wonderful. Then I can sort out these things and realize what other people are talking about, what they meant, sort of thing. I use it for jazz or folk music, that sort of thing. Can listen to various interpretations. Can play them off against one another and listen to them. I get a lot of them. And I find the computer so useful for finding out information. All sorts of esoteric things. Might spend an hour and a half, a couple of hours, on the computer. Or if it's bad weather and I don't want to walk up to the workshop, I'll listen in the afternoon. We've had a revelation this last week: got a friend who's developed dementia and it's so awful and sad to see. His wife doesn't have the slightest interest in music, but she is looking after him. Amazingly, I made a disc for him, a nice collection of music. And gave it to her and said, 'You'll find this helpful, he'll enjoy it.' And she took it home and had no idea what it was going to do for her husband. She rang up in shock yesterday. It had got through to him – it's very difficult to get through to him as the months go by, or even the weeks. He's needing supervision the whole time. When he has the music, he doesn't need it. She could go into another room and it would be OK.

It is more than likely that Bernard and Jeanette represent the future for older people, certainly for those who are now in their sixties, say, and who have already become used to new media. They will see how to fuse old and modern in new and creative ways; that being online and connected will actually facilitate rather than diminish their craft. It is digital media that will allow us to become hobbyists with specialist interests, even quite esoteric pursuits, as we will be able to source the special woods from Sweden or rare chemicals from China, or a missing piece of china from one's collection sourced through eBay from Hull: a future that may well see the English return to their eccentricities and obscure passions simply because they can.

That they refused to make claims for their ability to craft new media reflected an English modesty that can become quite a challenge for hospice staff. It was because she didn't want to be a problem that Jeanette was proving to be a problem. Notwithstanding her mastectomy two years previously, she kept insisting she didn't really need any help. There was no need to spend valuable hospice time visiting her and, when asked, it was always, 'I am just fine, thank you. No problems at all. You really don't need to bother ringing up and checking especially on a weekend.' As she put it:

> I felt from the outset that I can stand on my own feet here. I'm a very difficult person to help. I felt I didn't need hospice help, at any rate. Actually, I kept them away. I'd say, 'Oh, there's no need to come next month, or three months will be alright.' And the nurse rang me up on a Saturday afternoon about two or three months ago. And I said, 'Why are you ringing on a Saturday afternoon? You ought to be at home.'

But, of course, this wasn't true. She needed the drugs and had to admit that taking them was a terrible experience that left her weak and depressed. She had particularly avoided contact because she didn't want anyone to suspect that she was almost suicidal: 'And they wanted to help me, and so they put me in the way of the hospice. It wasn't actually what I needed. I needed a psychiatrist to understand that the hormonal disturbance was more than I could cope with.' The drugs had exacerbated a congenital problem that led to incessant pain and various other symptoms she would rather forget.

She recognizes these contradictions when we are talking about someone else, such as when her sister was desperately ill and refused to admit it. Jeanette freely agreed that one major advantage of the webcam was that when her sister was claiming she was just fine, Jeanette could literally see for herself this was entirely untrue. 'I could tell by her voice, but I needed the confirmation of seeing her. The webcam was in its infancy then. We could see her as well as listen to her, and then she didn't have to say anything. I could tell. I can see that the webcam would be very valuable to the staff looking after a patient.' As her sister was in New Zealand, it was always clear that the webcam was their best option. They used to speak for an hour a week when it was 9 p.m. on her Saturday night and 7 a.m. for her sister on Sunday morning. Jeanette's sister seemed more comfortable talking to her English sibling than to anyone in New Zealand. But then she was always that kind of English New Zealander. It wasn't just the illness that she failed to disclose. When she died, Jeanette found out about all sorts of accomplishment and prizes her sister had won that had never been mentioned while she was alive. This English modesty was engrained.

None of this, however, has made Jeanette herself any more likely to accept the care that she needs. The point, of course, is that you can have all the new media you like, but that does nothing at all to dislodge a patient's reluctance to disclose how they are really feeling.

Story 15

The Intimacy of Strangers

Behind this work with the hospice was our much larger project about the use and consequences of social media, called Why We Post. One of the most frustrating aspects of my research is the way people want to see new media as something apart from *real* life, a kind of *virtual*, online world that is intrinsically inauthentic. I usually respond with the following made-up anecdote:

A person overhears an hour's conversation between their friend and their friend's mother on the phone. After which they say, 'Gosh, that didn't sound good. What's your relationship with your mother like in the real world?' Of course, we would never say this. We have accepted the phone call as an integral part of our social relationships. The stories in this book suggest the same is just as true of new media. It is simply that they are less familiar than the traditional phone. I hope the point is 'nailed' in Helen's story. But Helen does more than this. Much of her story is about other, unprecedented, varieties of social contact that are only possible thanks to the internet. Her story shows why it is equally important to acknowledge and give credit to the reality of these new types of sociality.

I am about to have my fortieth birthday. I have one toddler, Alice, aged two. She has been able to use the phone since she was one and the iPad since she turned two. Scrolling through pictures, enlarging pictures, FaceTiming. Yesterday I was having a bath, put the iPad on the floor in the bathroom so she could watch *Peppa Pig*. So I'm in the bath and I say, OK, watch *Peppa Pig* on the TV, and she goes, 'It's not the TV. It's the iPad, Mummy.' So, yes, at two, she's very aware of what's going on. She recognized people by voice from before she was one – they do. I'm trying to think what age she started talking on the phone, probably about ten months. She was talking and walking. She's an incredible communicator, very, very good vocabulary for her age. She's so switched on, what she knows and understands. Children are growing up with all of this; the technology is there. A lot of people probably don't think it's necessarily a good thing, but they're going to grow up with that tech. Kids have iPads in the classroom. If it gives them an advantage, if she knows how to use it, then it's a good thing. She FaceTimes my sister, my nieces and nephews, who have iPods and iPads, and my sister has an iPhone.

I look at Facebook about twenty times a day. My husband would mainly put things up on my profile, jokes like, 'Oh, I've got the best husband in the world.' I won't put up a status very often. I am not one of those ones that does it every five minutes. Only if something is important. A lot of people will tell you when they're getting dressed and everything. It's only when something has happened I want to communicate with all my friends. Less than every couple of days. Put a photo up maybe once every couple of weeks. 'Like' something, probably five times a day. Comment probably a couple of times a day. Got lots of photo albums: all the wedding ones are on there, honeymoon, baby scans, everything. Open to friends, but not friends of friends. Put up my scan. I had some amazing ones, had one of her waving – could see her hand. Mainly get congratulations, I hadn't announced it. It was the first ultrasound.

I never announced anything about my illness on Facebook until after I finished treatment. But a few people I hadn't spoken to for years figured there was something wrong with me from my posts. I had put a few things on there that would insinuate there was a problem or something not going right. Liking a lot of things to do with breast cancer, or just saying things like I was proud of my husband; things like that – something going on there. And that prompted about five or six people to message me privately, 'Is everything OK?' And I only told the people who messaged me. Even my ex picked up something was wrong and messaged me. It was kind of – well, if people contact me and ask me about it, I'll tell them, but if you're not going to ask me about it, I'm not going to. It was a bit like that, you know.

Offline, my husband kind of forced it upon me. He texted my closest friend, saying 'You should contact Helen, she's had some bad news.' I hadn't heard from her in a while. And she sort of asked me how I was and everything. I put it on text, never actually spoke to her face to face. It was awkward. There was an element of feeling a bit embarrassed about it, sort of. I did feel that people who did know me would know there was something wrong or that I had not been in contact or whatever, and I kind of left it a little bit to other people to contact me. Because I just felt I had to concentrate on getting better, rather than worrying about other people or what they're thinking. I wasn't, you know, interested in their problems – couldn't deal with anything else. I literally wanted to be concentrating on me, my husband and my daughter really, and obviously my family who were supporting us. A lot of people don't know what to say. Some people don't say anything, which I think is worse. I'd rather someone put their foot in it than just didn't say anything.

Some of them are still messaging me every now and then, asking me how I am. I met this lady who also uses the hospice. At the hospital they asked, 'Can we put you in contact with her?' She had a different type of cancer but was also going through treatment at the same time, and so we started messaging each other. She got diagnosed the same time, she had her operation three days after mine, and we were on the same floor with the same surgeon, so I went to see her. I friended her on Facebook. She was putting things on Facebook about when she was having chemo and stuff like that. I never put anything about treatment or scans or anything. Was a bit awkward to begin with. I did say to her, 'Oh, well maybe I'll pop in,' but I didn't know it would be the same floor or whatever, and she was like, 'Oh, fine, Yeah.' I'm not quite sure, I don't want to intrude here, and she said, 'No, no, no, come in.' And it was, yeah, it was nice. We had a chat, exchanged a few stories, you know, about treatment and stuff. I was literally in the room. We hugged each other, said hello, met for the first time and one of the first things she did was show me her scars. 'Take a look at this,' she goes [laughs], lifting her gown up. I said, 'Oh, there's a story to be told with this. It looks like a bite! Maybe you can start telling people that.'

One of my sister's really close friends, his girlfriend got diagnosed as well, and I was friends with him but not her. So I then befriended her, and we spoke a little bit but there wasn't much communication between us. We did message each other a bit but I just found her really hard work. But she, again, was putting a lot of stuff on Facebook about treatment. Posting loads of pictures of herself, all made up and everything. That's great for her but that's just not me. Personally, I think they are doing it like a therapy, to tell someone or to say this is what's going on. A lot of things are done for show. So in her case, it's almost like she's got to keep up some sort of appearance. Could it even be a front? It might not even be how she's feeling at all; could just be to mask her real feelings.

I wanted it to be more private. I didn't want all of that everywhere. I didn't want to be that person. Just wanted to be me still. I think that goes back to what I was saying about embarrassment. That was one of the issues when I was going back to work, like, what are people thinking of me? Are they thinking I've got half a boob? What are they saying or thinking? Are they thinking I'm any less of a woman now? Ultimately, they're never going to find out and they can think what they like; it doesn't matter. But, again, someone asked me about it, someone from work. Like did they cut it from underneath? I'm quite happy to tell people when they ask me. I dropped Alice off at pre-school and one of the ladies knew I'd been ill, and she asked me about it. She sort of said her brother had had some sort of tumour or something. So straight away she's trying to establish the fact that I know a little bit about this sort of thing, you know, not the same thing, but I can sympathize, can understand her situation.

When I first got diagnosed, pretty quickly I did a search and I found the Bosom Buddies one, and also one that specializes in younger women under forty or who have young children. My child was one when I was diagnosed. And they're a private group and have a very strict criteria for joining because it's specifically just people going through treatment, being diagnosed. Then there are subgroups; can go off into different groups. I found it incredibly useful. I made a lot of virtual friends through that. If I had a question about anything, it would be the first place I'd go to because you get an instant response, absolutely instant.

And still it continues to be really good support. I probably go onto it every day. I see other women's posts that you may or may not comment on. I am not sure if this is normal or whatever but I actually put up my pathology report. I didn't openly put it on there. I asked a question and someone responded and offered to look at the report, so I privately messaged her and she kind of gave it back to me in laymen's terms so it was easier to understand. There's some ladies that sort of run the group. They are very strict on the privacy of the group. You know certain things you're not allowed to do on there. It's protection really from the outside. If you're asked to be a friend, you can know who they are. I'm friends with about five of them. Weirdly, someone that I knew offline was also on there.

There are cons to it, obviously – the amount of people that are in the group, there's about 500; big group. You do get people that don't make it. These posts that come up – this person passed away. Even if you haven't had dealings with that person, it's very sad and brings you back to reality. The first time I heard someone passed away, she was 32 years old, and that hit me quite hard. I was in the middle of treatment and I just thought this is just awful. It's just an awful, awful disease. And people do tend to think breast cancer, yes, you'll be fine. But young people are still dying of it. And they have a group for people that have secondaries.

Anonymity really helps when asking personal questions. You know, I had to go through a lot of hormone treatment. Kind of puts you into this sort of menopause; don't know if it's permanent or not. And it gave me the worst rages ever. I'd just be so, so angry. Had an injection which suppresses the hormones. I thought I was going mad. I can't control myself: awful, awful feeling. Maybe this is something you don't really want to discuss with your doctor or whoever. But put something like that on one of these Facebook groups, you will get plenty of women coming back and saying that's completely normal. That's what it can do – it's awful. We understand. Try this or that, it might help.

I started losing my hair; the first hair I lost was my pubic hair. And I was so shocked by it, wasn't prepared for it. I was complaining to my husband for shaving in the bath and not swilling it out, and I posted, 'Oh, my God – I've just lost all my lady garden!' And the amount of women who were like, yay, it's the first hair to go, and you sort of have a bit of a joke about it. You can't joke with just anyone about it, but you can if someone else is in the same situation.

You have to kind of be recommended. There was another girl from a different group who had said to me there is a group for younger women: why don't you try it? I'll recommend you for the group. You then have to answer a set of questions without knowing what the group is. You've just been told by someone from the group what you've got to tell them. Then someone looks at it and says, 'Yes, I'll add you.' There's other groups, different types of breast cancer, some different subgroups. There was a relationship one, just so people could go on and ask questions about their relationship. I think the lady who set it up is a lawyer; when she set it up, there wasn't anything like it. It's a fantastic idea, really.

Another subgroup they had was focused on the months of chemotherapy. So you could join a group that would be having chemo at the same time as you. So you are sort of friendlier with people having treatment at the same time as you. And then, when you have finished treatment, who can join the moving-on group, which I have. But you still look back at the other group, at the other people coming through or asking questions. And you keep track of what's going on, what they're doing, and stuff like that.

I was previously part of a forum – babies and bumps, something like that. This group of people all got together at roughly the same time, and I've kept in contact more with those people than with my NCT group which I don't hear anything from. We created our own Facebook account. A load of us joined it, and for a good year it was very active. Now I've probably got four or five women on my Facebook as friends from that group, who all have children the same age as my daughter. Not local. I don't see them. It is strange how you build up these relationships with people like that. It was a few of the women from that group clicked that there was something wrong with me and messaged me. And they would understand the way you showed anxiety and your language. You were pregnant; you had a bump. When you go through something with someone – babies or illness – you have something so great in common, more so than perhaps your best friend because your best friend may not be at the same stage.

You can be a lot blunter, more open to asking or making statements about things, than you would be with your own friends, the ones you see on a weekly basis. You might want to discuss something which you might not want your friend to know, or about your husband, but it doesn't matter; you're probably never going to meet them. One of the women in the group, her husband was having an affair. And she asked my advice. And I thought what should I be saying? I don't have that experience. But it doesn't necessarily have to be a moan or a gripe; it can also be that someone else has got knowledge I haven't got.

I've joined the moving-on group and it does get a bit much. Don't want it in your face all the time. I had to stop a lot of the feeds, otherwise every other thing was cancer, cancer, cancer, and I'm not moving on. Think I'll get rid of these off my Facebook. I would have to go and change the settings to say I don't actually want to see these unless they are a friend. I've answered probably twenty calls about life insurance. I've said I do not want you calling me. I'm already ill. I will never be able to get life insurance again. And they don't know what to say. You just want to get rid of them. I don't want to keep repeating myself. My sister thinks maybe I can't move on because of this.

I created a post when I finished my treatment. It was my last day of radiotherapy. I wrote it, ready to put onto my Facebook. Admitted it had been the worst year of my life, but I wanted to thank my family for being such brilliant support and my daughter who has also helped by being the light at the end of the tunnel – big smiles and lots of funny moments. She'll never know how she kept me going in fighting this. I didn't actually say I had cancer, but I got an awful lot of response from that, with people just saying, you know, you've been fantastic, been so strong. And that did spur a few more people to ask. It was kind of to say this is done and dusted now. I felt I did need to do it. And it was closure for me. Then later on I did put on an official announcement. I put, 'OK, I haven't announced this on Facebook; for the last eight months, I've been fighting breast cancer. Come out the other side. It hasn't been easy and if it wasn't for family I wouldn't have got through it. Looking forward to a future with my long-suffering husband.' Got many comments on that, a few from people who I never thought would actually make a comment, really old school friends, guys as well. One I had not really been in contact with since I was a child.

It's emotional, the same as when you announce your baby is born and get a lot of comments back on that. Same sort of emotion. My sister put: 'Total respect. Don't agree with Facebook, but what a strong beautiful woman you are.' Another: 'Really pleased it turned out positive but can imagine what you must have been going through.' Had that experience himself. I think his dad died from cancer. Someone just put kisses. 'So pleased for you. You're a credit to your family.' 'Great beautiful lady, must meet up soon; glad you're OK.' I got some flowers from work, from my team. I only got two get-well cards. I don't think people do get-well cards any more. Or is it because it's cancer? 'Sorry to hear you've got cancer. Get well soon.' I don't think they do cards like that.

Story 16

The Silent Community

These next two stories are pointers towards the conclusions. Vanessa, in her seventies, was one of the first patients we worked with. When walking towards her home, I remember that Maria and I were commenting on how this looked like the ideal setting for a close neighbourhood, the perfect community. In fact, it was the ideal interview for challenging our preconceptions. It made us wonder about what other assumptions we were making. For example, when it comes to people's local relationships, the problem may not be social change but rather the influence of past generations.

Vanessa has lived for more than fifty years in the hamlet of Purham. She arrived here following her marriage but was born in a nearby village. In terms of residence, the furthest she ever went from her place of birth was the other side of the hill where she lived for a short period. Her husband came to the area originally as an evacuee from London during the Second World War. This was a prime site for London evacuees and many hospice patients had stories regarding the impact of evacuees on the villages. The homes in Purham are unusually small and there are no clear divisions between them, so it as though the whole area is one garden with homes dotted around it. Walking around the village lanes, which are almost too small for cars, is an absolute delight. The dominant feature are garden gnomes. But not necessarily the 'traditional' Snow White gnomes with their Disney genealogy. Today, themes range from meerkats to dogs sporting handkerchiefs, whose main common feature is a friendly and slightly quirky humour. They seem appropriate for the miniature gardens surrounding each house with their immaculate flower beds and associated rockeries, trellis work, tiny lawns and compact water features, including fountains. This is one of those parts of England where you can still hear people conversing with a smattering of Latin terms, such is the degree of horticultural knowledge. Almost always, the best way to begin a discussion with a hospice patient in England is by complimenting them on some feature of their garden. This was not at all hard when it came to people living in Purham.

Vanessa and her husband share not only this small home but also several disabilities that come with old age, though only she has had cancer, which recently returned. Yet, typically for English people of her generation, when we ask how she is faring, she claims:

Oh, much better. I think I look better by the day really. I am getting better. Would you like a soft drink or anything? My legs were beginning to notice it so I didn't do too much yesterday. I thought I'd rest them a bit. But you've got to use your legs, haven't you, to get them better? It's no use sitting on the settee and hope they get better by themselves because they won't. They just get weaker. But I am feeling pretty good, yeah.

It transpires from our discussion that there have been some problems with the local hospital. It had recently lost some key information about her blood sugar and other records, staff had failed to attend the last visit they had scheduled, and therefore did not bring her the medicine she was expecting and needed. But, despite all this, she doesn't complain. This information is just matter-of-fact, a by-product of questions about who had visited her recently. The problems are compounded by the lack of joined-up care between the various institutions. We found it quite hard to disentangle who was coming on visits from the doctor's surgery, who from the hospital and who from the hospice, let alone all the differences between community nurses, district nurses and specialist cancer nurses. Vanessa was another of those patients who supported Marilyn's complaints about the lack of joined-up information between medical professionals.

In other respects, Vanessa at first sounds quite fortunate in that her immediate family live close by and she is not short of face-to-face contact. After her father's death, her mother came to live just opposite for 14 years, and her brother still lives just down the road. Vanessa also has a son living around the corner, and she particularly enjoys visits from her little great-grandchildren two or three times a week. Despite the bright and breezy tone of the conversation, in some ways it also took the shine off living in Purham. One sees the idyllic gardens, but none of the homes have more than two bedrooms and they are quite cut off from any facilities, such as shops, with very limited provision for parking. As is often the case, what seems quaint today speaks to the poverty of yesteryears.

Visitors are frequent, including recently Vanessa's grandchildren and brother, plus several visits from her nephew. It is almost all family; the only non-relatives are a friend of her brother and a friend of her niece. Vanessa dwells almost entirely on the great-grandchildren; how they played in the garden and with which toys. How the little five-year-old carefully made sure that the blanket was tucked in all around Vanessa, paying special attention to how it could be carefully folded around her neck. 'Didn't say a word. Just made sure I was comfortable. It does you just so much good.' Mind you, the three-year-old is a bit of liability, a real 'bull in a china shop,' picking leaves off the plants and a threat to all those little ornaments they cherish.

It is clear from other conversations that the younger generation often experience such visits as something of a trial. Given the generational distance, they assume their 'news' will be of little interest. They are therefore unsure what they should talk about when they visit. They become restless because they see themselves as rambling on about something just to pass the time, while the aim of their visit is to be polite, not rushed or giving the appearance of ill will.

They would probably be really quite shocked by the way Vanessa reports such visits. She has actually listened with rapt attention to every little detail. Vanessa can provide a full ten minutes' discussion, almost word for word, of how one such young visitor had been trying to buy a house, the difficulties in getting a mortgage and the results of the surveyor's reports and subsequent negotiations. And this for a friend of a relative whom they had never previously met and are unlikely to meet again. Vanessa can tell you everything about what happened between a grandchild and a teacher and their end-of-term report. With evermore limited possibilities to have any kind of experience herself, she retains, or even expands, her interest in others and feast on the crumbs of active lives with news to report, whatever that might be.

It would be easy to assume that the beauty of the gardens signifies an active community, with constant interaction between neighbours. But Vanessa states clearly that this is not the case. Mostly, neighbours are people they no longer get along with at all well. With the immediate neighbours, it is even worse. She suggests that some of them

> are absolute horrors. And if I were to tell the nice people, then the others will get to know as well, and I don't particularly want them to know my business. It's private. If they were nicer people . . . Chap who lives opposite there, his wife has just died and I'm very sorry for him, but he is an absolute pig. He writes letters to the ••••, telling them what he's been doing. And he writes letters saying that people's gardens are untidy and that they've been doing this and that and the other. There's one or two others that are a bit like that as well.

This is especially shocking as Vanessa was born in this area, went to school here and has lived here for more than 50 years. Yet her social life is entirely her family, and her lack of friendship with neighbours extends to the wider village. In discussing the community, she notes:

> I used to be a churchgoer a long, long time ago, but that sort of fell by the wayside. My husband is not a churchgoer. We did used to go to pubs when we were younger, but I'm not a drinker at all. Not because I have any morals about it or anything. It's just because it doesn't suit me. It just makes me feel ill so I don't see the point. My husband isn't either. He used to be a cricketer and a footballer and he would go out for drinks afterwards and things, but he didn't continue that after he finished,

the social side, because he's not really bothered about drink either. No.

The temptation is to imagine this is something new, the increasingly fragmented and individualized life of the modern world, compared to the more socialized past. In England, there is constant nostalgia for a supposed past when everyone was in and out of each other's homes, a time when people needed to borrow sugar and garden tools. But this nostalgia forgets the resentment people felt at that time for precisely this evidence of their dependency upon each other. This is why it is in these impoverished neighbourhoods that people find more solace in the autonomy of relative affluence. By ignoring or quarrelling with their neighbours, they show conspicuously that they no longer need them.

We are on neighbourly terms with a load of people up here, but we are not on friendly terms. There's a few difficult people round here, and I don't particularly want to broadcast it that I'm not well. We've got one lovely next-door neighbour but he spends most of his time in France. He's got a holiday – well, another home – in France, and he spends most of his time there. If I'm out in the garden, I won't stop talking to people going up and down the road, but I wouldn't call any of them my close friends.

In direct repudiation of the nostalgic view, Vanessa sees nothing new in all this. If there is an anti-social element that is coming across, she feels she inherited this from her parents.

I think it was my mum really. She was never really a mixer so we never really got into the habit of doing things like that. I never went to clubs or anything. I did use to go to the youth club in ••••. I remember that, but I wasn't the sort of person to join the Guides. Mum never would've thought of saying to me, 'Do you want to go to Guides?' because we're all sort of homebodies really.

They could easily have been at the centre of village social life. Her grandparents were local farmers and she was brought up in the house they had built. Vanessa's father was both a local grocer and a policeman. He became a sergeant and was very proud of this role. But that was the problem – the pride. Both her mother and father were devoted to becoming and remaining respectable, and the dominant mode of respectability came through considering oneself just slightly above and aloof from those who lived in close proximity. In striving to be a little bit better, one came to regard the people living close by as just a little bit worse, those who by association would act as a drag upon this drive to improve oneself. 'Mum was really into respectability, yes. I had a friend who lived just along the road and his mother was divorced and my mum really frowned on that. You don't get divorced. Look at the poor Queen: she's got three children divorced, hasn't she, out of four. But in those days it was quite a stigma to be divorced.'

The upside to this devotion to local respectability is that it kept the family close, which in turn gives Vanessa the blessing of constant face-to-face visits during the week. Her parents looked askance at the idea of family members moving to other areas. 'My mum was terrified of London, basically. Yes, it was like going to a foreign country to go to London at that time.' In order to visit the city, Vanessa and her brother had to make friends with some relatives of her grandmother 'because they were quite confident going on the trolley buses and going round

London.' Listening to Vanessa, one is reminded that many scenes in Jane Austen's novels are set in an area at precisely this distance from London. Today, it is a half-hour drive, but then it was a 20-year wait before one's first visit.

Visually, Purham is exactly the site that someone who was trying to engineer a social community might have created. The very fact that you have to walk, rather than drive, along the narrow paths between these small houses seems to create the perfect conditions for neighbourliness. Vanessa herself is a well-meaning, evidently decent, person who gets on well with most of her family. Yet it is clear that the intense observations of neighbours at a social level leads only to a litany of slights and complaints. So how can we reconcile all this with the evidence from the gardens? I would call this a 'silent community'. If you were to carefully map the features of the gardens of Purham, it would be evident just how much attention each person pays to their neighbours. The distribution of flowers, such as a type of rose or the presence of camellias, is not equally spread. They tend to cluster because people are very aware of what their neighbours have done to their gardens and will readily 'borrow' good ideas. The same intensity of observation that leads them to keep their distance means they are exceedingly aware of what their neighbours are doing and may often be very influenced by them. They observe and copy but they don't actually talk.

To be fair, in the case of Vanessa, there are other more personal factors. Her mother also suffered from a rather unpredictable manic depression, which in turn afflicts Vanessa's own daughter, Nicola. When she is well, Nicola is very helpful, especially now Vanessa's husband isn't allowed to drive for health reasons. But at other times, the care is the other way around. The last time that Nicola moved house seems to have been especially problematic, sending her into such deep depression that their son-in-law found he couldn't get her out of bed and had to take time off work in order to look after her. As a result, they fell into rent arrears. So they came to live with Vanessa and her husband for two years. The couple took the bigger bedroom, Vanessa stayed in the smaller one and her husband in any case prefers to sleep in a reclining chair since he has problems with his back and shoulder. This was six years ago, and they had to develop a rota system around the family, because Nicola had developed suicidal tendencies and couldn't be left alone. Typically, Vanessa never talks about her cancer in terms of personal affliction, but argues that it was extremely sad to discover a few months back that the disease had returned because of the consequences of that development for the core task of looking after Nicola.

In talking with hospice patients there is often a clear trajectory. People are phlegmatic and try to remain upbeat. It takes a while before the more troubling elements emerge. At first, the overwhelming impression is of Vanessa's close family support. But then, as in the case of Nicola, the individual members of the family start to emerge in a more ambivalent light. An example is Vanessa's brother. In early conversations, the talk is all about how her brother comes to visit and brings his friend. But, as Vanessa opens up, she admits that things are not so straightforward. In fact, her brother had retired which made him enormously important in helping both Vanessa and her daughter. But then, much to everyone's surprise, quite recently this brother took on a new job. Vanessa confides that she thinks it was directly connected with the new diagnosis and the return of Vanessa's cancer. Her brother had been running around trying to help everyone but really couldn't cope. Vanessa feels that the main reason her brother has found some employment was to legitimate a withdrawal from that caring role. Vanessa doesn't believe this was a conscious decision, simply something that he needed to do under these difficult circumstances, which of course has made everything much worse. It was simply easier for her brother to take employment, even at his advanced age, than to admit to the others that he was struggling to provide this level of care. Fortunately, Vanessa's nephew has to some degree stepped into the breach.

Beyond the family, there is a paucity of friends locally. But there were friends who Vanessa had come to know through work, and who have since developed into what she thinks of as her 'email friends'. But, as her illness has progressed,

> you do begin to realize that maybe I've got to think differently. Because if I'm going to be incapacitated, in whatever way, you know you've got to think around – and I mean I've literally not been able to send people emails. I've managed to just open them perhaps, and then it's 'Oh, my back'. I may have to think around these issues for myself. So it's quite useful to have this discussion.

For many patients, relationships are not just with people but may be with pets, homes and even with cancer itself. Vanessa has had this close relationship with cancer for some fifteen years now. As with many close relationships, it has become a hub around which all sorts of other relationships have developed. Through cancer, she came to have a much closer relationship with her sister-in-law, who already had cancer and has become the main person of whom Vanessa could ask questions about what was likely to happen. Then there are the key nurses, including the hospice nurses, some of whom she has known now for a decade. There is also her local GP and others who care for her. Not all of these are reliable, but none of them play around the way cancer itself seems to have done. She has become mouse to a cancer cat. One moment she is released, as a mastectomy is supposed to have cleared the disease and she doesn't even appear to need chemotherapy. Then there is a virulent attack on some other organ that threatens to destroy her but which is finally overcome. Cancer may leave her alone for months, or even years, but then returns with tragic force. In the end, the cat will always end its play with the death of the mouse, but who knows how long that game will continue?

Story 17

In This Room

Harold, in his eighties, was one of our final interviewees. His story confirmed that parochialism was no bar to isolation. As well as that rather shocking finding, it was with Robin that we first encountered how often it is commercial contacts that remain when other social contacts have fallen away, in this case through adding the perspective of his gardener, Geraldine.

Harold was born in this room, in this bed, and it is in this same bed, in the same room, that he will die. In this room you can see some of the finest furniture that Harold ever made. It is, in truth, a dark little room, and the dark varnish of his furniture only seems to add to the feeling that much has been absorbed, but little has been reflected, as things have shrunk back to the small space that is left of his life. The thick net curtains are now a barrier to anything that lies beyond. The room speaks to a word they used at the time of his birth: his mother's 'confinement'. It would then have been a cosy room, suitable to give birth in. Today, he hardly goes out of the room, let alone the house. Of course, he ventured forth in all those years in between, but it was always to a relatively restricted world. He never worked further afield than the local town.

But what the room lacks in breadth, it gains in depth. It was these walls that reverberated with the very earliest memories that we encountered in this research. Harold's very elderly mother could tell tales of her own grandparents that led us back to a period that now seems timeless. She was born in her own grandmother's house in what was in those days just a little hamlet, a place that would have been barely noticed since this was a Georgian landscape, dominated by the great houses and estates. Her grandfather:

> used to work on the farms. He used to take hay carts and horses to London. Told me he'd have a few pints on the way and the horse used to know his own way back. Harold's father's father, the other grandfather, he was a famous balloonist, a captain, was well known for pioneering airships. When I was about eight or nine, I came up the village with my grandmother and in those days it's the old bonnets and long skirt, horse and carriages, not cars, and all the women used to work in the big houses in service. Things like that. I was by the church walking and this carriage and pair came trotting up the village with this gentry in it. Went to the kerb as they went passed and curtsied, and I remember saying to myself, I'm not going to do that when I grow up. That's how it was, if you didn't do that, you lost your job. Had to be subservient to them. Otherwise you was out of work, didn't have any work or anything to go to.

Harold recalled:

> a narrow lane that led into a farm at the end. And the big field at the back was converted into the airfield in the war. Only school I went to, little flintstone school. Just a little elementary school. My

father got me a job when I was 14, that pub – used to be packed when we used to be there. They used to come from miles around. Usual thing, little village. Was a lot of bartering going on: poachers, rabbit catchers, would come and sell the rabbits up there, anything anyone wanted. Was always someone there. Someone would be able to do it.

Harold worked, but his devotion remained to his house and garden, to which his contribution over the years is very evident.

Up the top of the garden I've got quite a well-equipped workshop, which I've gathered together over the years. I made that fireplace, made that from a cabinet which I must finish, TV table – that tray – that table, I can go on and on. Always been for ourselves. I don't make stuff to sell. Kitchen was the last thing I did. But because I was getting ill, we had to cheat a bit and we bought the kitchen cabinet and I made all the doors and everything else to go on it. So, personal on the outside and modern on the inside.

But 'All the people we knew then have died now. So, I mean, you can understand that there aren't many left our age. Knew quite a few people. Don't write letters now. Used to write them. But, you know, I haven't got anyone really.' The sheer lack of contacts was made clear to Harold by a recent incident. As so often in these villages, when someone gets ill, Harold's neighbours said 'anything you want, give us a knock,' but he has never done that. Yet it was the neighbours who recently saved Harold's wife:

When my wife fell over last week, she was lying there, no one about, couldn't get up, about 8 p.m. at night or something like that. Was on the lawn. She was there about half an hour. We don't have a lot to do [with the neighbours], say hello, this side next door, never spoke. But he was watching TV– football – and he came out at half-time to have a smoke. And he found [Harold's wife], went and got his wife, brought her in. I had gone up the road. When I came back, she was sitting waiting for the ambulance to come. My wife said to me, 'I didn't think I liked that woman, but she was very nice.' Need someone to break the ice. He had heard her calling so he had come straight round. He got through the side gate which was open. Was glad he was here, blimey. Was there till I come back. They keep asking how she is. I always did get on all right with them myself, but my wife, she didn't get on, she didn't push herself. Know what I mean. But they started coming forward, being shy. Been here about a year, not long; only rent the place I think. They're middle-aged. Got a young family. Got two girls and a boy, all at school.

But that was exceptional because Harold repeats what has become a common refrain:

There's a lot of people out there who have said if you need any help, give us a call, so they're offering the help. But not actually coming in and seeing me. Probably want to have a chat when I go outside. Yeah, people don't like to intrude. I mean, because with me this illness has come on so quick. I imagine they're finding it a bit difficult to handle what's happening to me. You know, daren't ask really.

One of the reasons was that, as Harold notes, he was 'never part of organizations. Bit of a loner like that. No, never been a sports person. Well, that's telling lies. I did do archery. And we got very good at it, which was part of its downfall, you know. That we got too good and everybody wanted us to be shooting while we just wanted some peace in our lives.'

In this respect, Harold was typical of many of the patients living in a village locality. There was however one exception. A domain within which they had been unusually sociable:

> We own a caravan, and we've got a district association. Used to go away virtually every other weekend, always emailing each other 'what's going to happen here?' You know, we don't go far. Furthest we'll be going is a place near Northampton. So never very far away. On a good day, we would have had about ten caravans, which is quite small. Got to know those people pretty well. Yes, they will bend over backwards to help me.

But even with respect to this community, when we asked if they now visit, Harold replied:

> No, not really, unless I was in desperate need. They would always know when we go, because obviously I'm very restricted on what I can do. Up to last year, took the caravan on back of the car, drove to wherever we're going, put the feet down and go and get the water, put the awning up. I always used to do that. So when I couldn't, one of the guys would go off and get the water for us. And they kept coming over saying, 'You alright? Need any help?'

But this ceased once Harold became confined to his home since they don't actually visit and he doesn't tell them how much he now does need their help.

So this is the question that we will need to confront. How we had wrongly assumed that a person who has lived in the same village all their lives would, at the time of being diagnosed with a terminal condition, have community and family support? One of Harold's children does live in the same village but rarely comes to visit him. They mainly communicate by phone. The last time he had seen either of his other children was three months earlier. As for the next generation, they had no desire to remain so confined. Common for low-income families, their route out of the village was through the army. But that meant the grandchildren were far away and, having moved before the days of modern communication, they had never really developed close bonds. There are several grandchildren but if Harold gets a visit once a month he counts himself fortunate, and they don't even phone much. One came to see her grandmother in hospital after that accident in the garden. Emails are so rare that Harold at first says he barely bothers to look, but then he knows this is also partly his own reluctance to embrace new media. It turns out that Harold does take a peek every other day and, for all his protestations, there is obvious disappointment when there is nothing new to see.

The situation is quite different if Harold goes out into the public domain. There are his caravanning friends but also those at the local pub.

> But if I do go now, like with my son-in-law, I think I don't know anyone. Yet, as soon as I go anywhere, it's, 'Oh hello, Harold!' I was well known and people do know me. In the surgery, full of people. When I go in it's, 'Oh, hello Mr ••••'. I said the other day, 'I wanted to see if you had a spare room up here at the surgery, save me coming up.'

If Harold goes to local shops, or indeed anywhere in the village, people know him. There is plenty of social engagement within the public domain. But, and it is a very big 'but', no one wants to intrude; no one wants to actually knock on the door and take a step into Harold's private business, and dying of cancer is quite embarrassingly private business. What do you say to someone who is dying? Better to say nothing at all than say the wrong thing. We come back again to that refrain: how they would all help if Harold asked them, but Harold, like many others, would perhaps literally 'rather die' than actually ask them.

Even when it is suggested they might go to the hospice, Harold can't accept that as an offer of help or support. At most, he can concede that they might pay a visit as his wife Sally would like to see the gardens, which are rather beautiful. As with so many older people in England, when their social relations become attenuated, they cultivate their plants instead. And this, perhaps not surprisingly, is how Harold came to find his final village friend. With cancer came complications, and eventually Harold simply couldn't continue with the gardening. But the garden had become central even to his marriage since it was axiomatic that Harold contributed his labour while Sally provided the enthusiastic appreciation. She loved gardens but had no more skill in propagation than Harold had for cooking.

When eventually Harold had to give up gardening, there was no doubt about where he would go for support. Geraldine and her husband were the village gardeners. When Harold approached Geraldine, it was only gardening he had in mind. But Geraldine had realized for quite some time that elderly people in the village generally hired her only ostensibly to look after their gardens. Typically, rather than being allowed to get on with that job, their employers would then insist that they come in for a cup of tea. They had by now dealt with many villagers who, like Harold and Sally, had lived there most of their lives but were now feeling isolated and lonely. Gardening was one of the most obvious and simplest ways to have another human being come to one's house for any length of time, and in any case talking about gardening had always been one of the main ways the villagers cultivated friendships, as much as plants.

While Geraldine concentrated as much as she could on the garden, inevitably her husband was asked in to resolve various DIY problems: putting up a curtain rail, changing a light bulb or setting up a new television were common requests, even though technically he too had come to help with the garden. In fact, these days they were increasingly being asked for help with people's difficulty in using their computers, but this was entirely beyond them. As they reported it, the expectation was that they would spend perhaps half their employed time just sitting having tea and being the human company that otherwise was so absent from the lives of these villagers. Geraldine recalls how:

One lady, whose garden we did for 20 years, sold her lovely bungalow on the estate and moved into a flat. She still phones me up about every couple of weeks to see how I am and we get together for lunch or a cuppa. In fact, really for a lot of people the cup of tea and the chat is the highlight. It's a bit incidental that they get the garden done. There's one lady, she's on her own and she's a friendly lady, but she hasn't got any friends. We're her friends, really; it's very sad. We've often said to people that in a lot of ways we feel like social workers. You know, we're a sort of link. Some of them almost look on you as family because they haven't got family. One of the ladies used to work and live on our road; her friends were the shopkeepers. I think that's important, if you stay in and don't see anyone.

This particular lady . . . her next door neighbours are very good. The woman will pop in and see her. But, apart from her, we're the only ones she sees or who go into the house. Sometimes when we do this particular lady (she's 88), we've just agreed to do the mowing. I do the edging and the weeding, and then she'll call us in for a cup of tea, and she will just keep nattering to me, and my husband will say, 'Oh, I'll go out and start the mowing now.' In a way, she doesn't want me to go back out. Just telling me medical problems, you know. Husband passed away a few years ago. She used to go and visit his sister, who moved away for whatever reason. They haven't been in contact much since. People have family, but they don't get on; not just that, they've moved away, but they say they haven't spoken to so-and-so for 20 years. Seems quite common that there are family issues. This other lady we work for, she's got two sons with high-powered jobs. And we always felt they didn't do enough. And, I'm sure she would agree, she sort of counts us as family. Because her family, two sons and they both have two children, busy lives. If we're there and they want us to do something, we charge by the hour. They pay us because it would encompass what we do while we're there. But if my husband goes down to do a special little thing, we won't charge.

So when Harold and Sally asked Geraldine and her husband to come and help with the gardening, they were actually quite surprised that the gardeners themselves seemed to assume that a new friendship was somehow part of the agreement. Geraldine was experienced enough to know that just because Harold was born in the same house that he will die in, just because there were three children and quite a few grandchildren and just because so many people in the village know him, none of this means that now, when he most needs it, he will have the friendship, the support and the company in the house where from now on he will spend most of his time.

Story 18

Matt

The final story in this volume is not anonymized. We made a short film about Matt Marshall as part of our Why We Post project which you can watch on YouTube.[4] Matt was keen to help our project since he himself worked in media and he was also active in helping to raise funds for the hospice. The film starts as follows:

I'm Matt Marshall. 41 years of age. I grew up in Yorkshire, Bradford and went to university in the Midlands and then came south. I've been living in this area now for 19 years. My priority is to keep a good work/life balance. I like to socialize down the pub with my friends, play football, go out of an evening. I'm quite driven at work, very ambitious. And then, obviously, that all changed.

Matt had realized something was wrong for quite some time, but his symptoms were initially misdiagnosed as indigestion. So he was completely unprepared for the meeting when he was informed that he had cancer of the oesophagus and that

---

[4] https://youtu.be/jVznhtV8MTI

they were 'very sorry to tell you, you have advanced cancer, which at this point is untreatable, beyond treatment, inoperable, therefore by definition terminal'.

Nine days after receiving this diagnosis he decided to post something on Facebook:

I knew I was ill. I knew there was something seriously wrong, if I admit it now, but there was an element of denial as well. I made an announcement, globally if you like, to my friends on Facebook. I thought, well, this is the best way to do it. One hit, you know. If I was getting engaged, or married, or had a baby, it'd be straight on there. This is equally important news, but negative. Making the announcement made it real. I was in denial. I'd played 90 minutes of football two days before I was diagnosed, even though I was having trouble eating. So when I was diagnosed, I thought, OK, I might die: 30 per cent chance. Survival rate is 16 per cent [after five years] but look at me, I'm fine. And I had my head in the sand, so making the announcement made it real. It brought it home to me. Writing it and posting it – when I pressed 'post', I was in tears. It became real, all became very real.

Matt was equally unprepared for the flood of supportive comments that came back from this and they clearly did matter.

One key moment in this trajectory was the referral by his GP to the hospice. Many people during this project noted that, since the hospice is seen (mistakenly) as synonymous with being terminal – a place you go into but will not return from – it is in itself a frightening prospect. It is only when they go there that they gain the reassurance that this is not necessarily what hospice care represents. Matt recalled being in tears before he first walked through the door: 'Shit. It's come to this. As soon as

Matt Marshall
July 11, 2013

Dear Friends - it is with great regret that i have to share this bad news with you - however Facebook appears to be a one hit catches all approach.
On Tuesday of last week i was diagnosed with cancer
I have a huge battle ahead of me. if you are so inclined prayers are welcomed - but good wishes and fingers crossed will mean just as much to me.
I hope to see you all at some point soon - and definitely to celebrate with you once this evil disease is beaten x

Like Comment Share   👍 34 💬 191

34 people like this.

View previous comments   50 of 191

on Kin 'ell
at 8:40pm · Like

t Sorry to hear that mate.You can beat it.

Figure 1 Matt's first posting about his cancer on Facebook

I heard *hospice*, I said no, no, no. I'm young and fit. The words "palliative care" I don't want to hear. I didn't want to accept it.'

In fact, there were potential treatments. 'At first, surgery wasn't guaranteed, chemo had to facilitate surgery. If it didn't shrink, I wasn't going anywhere.' So he began his course of chemotherapy.

Later still, he posted, 'Chemotherapy Session 3 of 3: all is progressing well and all the indicators are that the naughty little tumour WILL BE operable. This will be confirmed in 3–4 weeks' time. So fingers are all crossed. Looking forward to the New Year – and a new chance at life. Have a great weekend everyone. x'

This was rather more upbeat than he actually felt. Matt had been unable to eat solid foods for months now, surviving on a sort of warm milkshake that he hated. Indeed, since the

Figure 2 'Chemotherapy Day One – or as I like to think of it . . .
The first day of the rest of my life!!! Bring it on x'

subsequent operation removed a section of his oesophagus, he
knew he would never be able to eat entirely normally again.

I attended a wedding on Facebook. Was supposed to be best man
but I couldn't travel. It was in August so they took live pictures. I

Figure 3 'The poor dog cannot understand why he cannot jump up on my knee.'

felt like I was included.' Facebook had also become a key determinant of the depth and nature of Matt's friendships. There were people he thought he barely knew who responded in ways he would never have expected, for example, by bringing him a sack of what they had been told were appropriate vitamins. In another case, a Facebook friend turned out to be a chemotherapy nurse, which he hadn't known, and that nurse sent him some very helpful literature. However, as noted in previous stories, one of the downsides of Facebook is its use of targeted advertising. 'If I'm putting oesophageal cancer, care, need, dietary requirements, I'm going to start getting blasted by online ads on my Facebook of things I don't want to see. I don't want to be reminded on a daily basis. I've gone through days and days after chemo before they could scan me, there were huge chunks of days where I forgot I was ill, which was fantastic. Last thing I need is that constant reminder, though. Don't want that automated advertising that has no feelings.

Figure 4 An image posted by Matt on his Facebook wall
Reproduced courtesy of ihadcancer.com

Although an extremely difficult experience, the chemotherapy went sufficiently well that Matt was eligible for surgery. After which he posted: 'Goodbye intensive care – I do not miss you at all. And quite frankly, if I never see u again, it will be too soon!!! Surgery went well and I am now in mending mode. Thanks for all your support and kind wishes. See you in the New Year y'all x'

Later still, he felt able to post:

Dear Friends – Firstly, thank you for all your support and best wishes through what has been a very testing time for me. Your support has helped me massively and kept me strong through some very low points.

Matt Marshall
November 19, 2013 via BlackBerry

Goodbye Intensive Care - I do not miss you at all. And quite frankly if I never see u again. It will still be too soon!!! Surgery went well and I am now in "mending" mode. Thank you all for your support and kind wishes. See u in the New Year y'all x

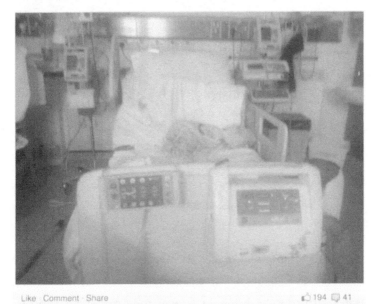

Like · Comment · Share   👍 194 💬 41

Figure 5 A photograph posted by Matt of his intensive care bed

And ... more importantly, the best wishes and prayers have worked! Today i received the news that my tumour has shrunk to a point where surgery is now possible – and the cancer has NOT spread!!!

There's a long way to go but it is fantastic news and i can now look forwards to a fair old shot at a long and happy life. Thank you all again – and hope to see you at a celebration party in the New Year.

Figure 6 A mirror selfie posted after recovery from chemotherapy

Matt returned to Yorkshire to recover and finally he felt able to show himself again to the world by posting a selfie as his cover photo on Facebook (see Figure 6).

Yeah, that was taken in my mum's bathroom three and a half weeks after surgery. I thought I looked bloody well. Just before the fourth week. I'd been out and walked a mile on the sea front. Which I had been told was not going to happen for 6–8 weeks. And I had been on this accelerated recovery programme. I was one of their youngest patients. One of the fastest to recover and get out, even though I think they discharged me a couple of days too early, looking more at the record than my health, but to be out and walking literally 23 days after having surgery and dying on the table, I thought good. And I had a rosy glow on my face from the fresh air. I was eating again; food, I was eating a lot, small and often, and it was real food, and it made me look a bit better anyway . . . To all intents and purposes, had you not known, I don't think you'd have known I was ill from that photo. So that's what I wanted to show. I was stood up, and I had some colour in my cheeks. I still had my hair. All was good with the world.

We planned for more interviews, but despite having been told that he was clear of it, Matt's cancer returned. He deteriorated rapidly and, sadly, he passed away.

Matt noted several times that posting on Facebook was just as much a means to acknowledge to himself his experience of the disease and anticipated recovery as it was about telling other people. Why end this book with a selfie? It is because the use of the selfie has come to be seen as superficial and narcissistic. Yet here we can see that a selfie represents a profound reflection of Matt's use of Facebook. This is not just a selfie; it is a mirror selfie, which in this particular context has become the perfect technology to succinctly express the simultaneous process of self and public acknowledgement. Whatever the technologies, we will find people who have creatively appropriated them in interesting and significant ways.

Indeed, every story in this book has been an instance of how people creatively appropriate the possibilities provided by life. Which is why any and every one of the fifty patients could have provided the material for a story. It was only the require-ments of editing for publication that prevents this volume being comprehensive in that sense. We encountered no uninteresting people. In this lies our fundamental equality and the reason we should support the hospice movement in helping all their patients gain and retain that sense of self-respect, not through praise in obituaries but while they are still with us.

Conclusions

Friendship

When it comes to the comfort of people, there are many potential sources of support and comfort from friends. Chrissie's (5) story sounds a bit like something from *Sex in the City*, or *Girls*, TV serials about four inseparable women, who in her case provide wonderful support. The wider ethnography confirmed just how common it has become for the friendships developed during ante-natal classes, or though mother and toddler groups, to become the most lasting friendships of later life. Sometimes it is common interests, as for Herbert (4) where it's an aesthetic appreciation that connects him to other people. More difficult is the legacy of people's working lives. This is sometimes the basis for strong friendships. Herbert (4) tells how forty or fifty of his ex-pupils have been in touch. Yet Emma (10) shows the other side of this coin, noting that although she has taught in the same school for 30 years, she has never developed the kinds of relationship that could spill out into this private domain. Veronica is equally upset about the lack of human interest from her employers at the National Health Service. Similarly, an informant, not present in this book, notes that around half of her Facebook friends come from work but that this rarely translates to people visiting her at home. Is the problem one of creating deeper social relations within large corporate or state institutions, or is it something to do with difficulties that the English have in developing deeper relationships more generally?

An even more ambiguous source of friendship is neighbours, who will be discussed in more detail later on. Suffice it to say that while neighbours are often listed as close friends, they are equally regarded as highly problematic and as people to be kept at a distance. Vanessa (16) illustrates how it is often low-income households, those who have always lived close to their neighbours, who are most likely to resent them. Stephen and Jackie (11) show how much this depends upon particular circumstances. One finding that has been common in my prior ethnographic studies is the sheer predictability of a kind of spatial determinism. People tend to be close to neighbours when they live in cul-de-sacs and not close when they live on through-roads. Not surprisingly, those such as Elizabeth (13) who spent a considerable time cultivating relationships with neighbours, for example, organizing annual street parties, will in turn gain the most support from those neighbours, though community memory may be short and people move frequently.

The wider ethnography of The Glades shed considerable light on this question of community. In brief, it became clear that most villages have a robust and thriving community at their core, hosting a very wide range of activities, some for the young, such as scouts and sports, and many for the retired, such as bowls, or amateur theatre and philanthropy such as the Rotary Club or the Lions. There is a clear pattern of involvement. Mothers with young children taking time off work are extremely likely to take advantage of the most local facilities. By contrast, it is relatively rare for working people to have much involvement at all in village life, unless they are in some sense 'activists'. For Stephen and Jackie (11), it has been working as Labour Party activists that left a legacy of friends, while for Elizabeth it was a concern for ecology reflected in the transition town movement. As people move from work to retirement, they often take on activities that are simultaneously philanthropic but also deliberately designed to prevent subsequent isolation. This often includes volunteering for the hospice, as a driver, in the case of Richard (13), or working in a hospice shop in the case of his wife. For some, this represents a longer-term commitment since Celia (8) was involved in volunteering throughout her life and Gerald's (9) social life is centred on his role as a leading citizen in his village. It is, however, rather more common for people to take up volunteering only upon retirement, though the level of such subsequent volunteering is prodigious.

Taken as a whole, though, community activities even amongst the retired tended to involve the same core group of, at most, a few hundred villagers. By contrast, the majority of people who live in these villages have only a minimal participation in any local activities, and then as users, not helpers. It was quite clear that for most villagers there is no such thing as community. This may be true even if they have lived in the same village for their entire lives. There is barely any mention of the Church in this book except Gerald's (9) insistence on preserving its role in the proper structure of society, and Elizabeth (13), who recounts how prayers were being said for her health. There were other patients (whose stories do not appear here) for whom the Church was enormously important and represented an entire community in and of itself, but once again they are a very small proportion of the whole. The Church may, however, be central to organizing activities for elderly patients such as Betty and Gloria (6).

Throughout these stories, there is a common acquiescence in stereotypical views about gender, where it is females who are viewed as the more naturally social and men as less able in this respect. The most explicit examples are perhaps Gerald's (9) somewhat dismissive characterization of what he nevertheless regards as the necessary background 'buzzing' of female social conversation, or Robin's (7) incapacity to sustain even a phone call in his own right.

The advent of illness may either extend these trends or bring its own ambiguities or reversals. The most striking new source of sociality comes from those now bound closely to people, essentially because they have the same disease, people with whom they feel able to talk directly about what is happening to themselves without embarrassment or explanation. This seemed especially prevalent for patients with breast cancer, such as Emma (10) and Elizabeth (13). Some prefer to meet these others, some to communicate without meeting, and some prefer the complete anonymity that is possible within website groups. On the other hand, there are those who feel it would diminish their lives to be over-identified with the disease and therefore, if anything, prefer to keep away from those with whom they only have an illness in common.

Finally, with regard to friendship more generally, a common finding is that those who are most present when one becomes a terminal patient are not necessarily those one might expect. Elizabeth and Richard (13) are quite disappointed by the behaviour of their best friend who seems to have faded into the distance. Many others talk of people avoiding them when they hear about the illness and simply not knowing how to respond. But there are plenty of counter-examples, such as Veronica (2) whose best friend comes through for her just as she expected she would.

The problem of Englishness

Unexpectedly, a single issue seems to emerge from this research, standing out as both the most surprising result and the one that demands more detailed analysis and explanation. How is it that we found people who were born, worked, lived and are now dying in the same rural setting but who nevertheless appear both lonely and extremely isolated? This finding emerged almost vicariously from our systematic trawl through each mode of communication in turn to see who patients were connected with. Particularly poignant were cases where the informant was insisting that they did indeed talk with others. But detailed investigation revealed that those others were merely commercial contacts. For example, Robin (7) told us that his wife, who is his carer, has regular face-to-face conversations but it turned out this was because she went once a week to have her hair done and talked to her hairdresser. Another informant also gave a business link as evidence for continued socializing, otherwise, he said, 'I wouldn't see anybody. I'm not interested. I'm just a loner.' Geraldine (17) is clear that being a village gardener is as much about being hired as company for the lonely as looking after flowerbeds.

This lack of support was often as true of family as of friends. One patient noted, 'My brother. Not in contact with him. I saw him last year, I think. His son's wedding. But I haven't forgiven him for my parents.' Robin says of his son, 'He comes around for Sunday lunch once a month and that saves a lot of bother.

He lives with a partner who has three children by her previous husband.' The grandchildren 'come round for various occasions like Easter Day or Christmas Day'. With regard to family in general, he says, 'We don't wish to impose. We avoid it. If they need help, I'd go to any lengths to do it. But generally speaking we don't interfere.'

Consider Harold (17) who has lived his entire life in this village and retained an active social presence outside with people with whom he had gone caravanning and camping. But with regard to how many people visit him at home, he says:

> In practical terms, probably only a couple. But there's a lot of people out there who have said if you need any help, give us a call. So they're offering the help. But for actually coming in and seeing me. Probably they want to have a chat when I go outside. Yeah people don't like to intrude. I mean because with me, this illness has come on so quick, I imagine they're finding it a bit difficult to handle what's happening to me. You know, daren't ask really.'

Despite the assertive way patients claim they don't want or need help and like their own company, it becomes clear that they are lonely and would dearly love more company if only there was some way this could arise without breaking the social norms that make it impossible. Dealing with PLS, Stephen and Jackie (11) have extremely difficult problems. But once again, while asserting that of course their neighbours would help, the last time that Jackie actually asked for practical assistance was three years ago when Stephen had a car accident and she had an operation and it was just impossible for them to drive.

These findings from interviews with patients were supported by my interviews with the hospice staff who contributed some even more extreme stories about children not turning up for their parents' funerals. Whether working with churches, pubs or welfare services, the findings from my eighteen-month ethnography of The Glades were consistent with these findings. It is therefore not surprising that similar results are encountered in broader national surveys. The UK Secretary for Health gave a speech on 18 November 2013 at the National Children and Adult Services conference on 'The Nation's Shame of the Forgotten Elderly', citing sources suggesting there are 800,000 people in England who are chronically lonely.[5]

Neither my evidence nor wider surveys suggest that this is usually the case. Most people do have support, but those who don't are a substantial minority. Victor and Bowling (2012: 326) suggest around 20–25 per cent of the elderly could be considered chronically or persistently lonely. This tends to result from much longer-term patterns of sociality that have become established for these individuals (Dahlberg, Andersson and Lennartsson 2016). Both conclusions would seem close to the generalizations one might make based on the present volume. A recent report by Relate (Sherwood, Kneale and Bloomfield 2014: 31) confirms the problems that English people may have in making friends which lead to around 10 per cent claiming they have no friends at all. So we are dealing with a minority but, given the rural setting, a surprising proportion of people whose social relations are now sparse.

The paradox is that alongside these findings regarding loneliness, there is much in this volume that would confirm the same informants' positive image of the contemporary English village

---

[5] http://www.bbc.co.uk/news/uk-politics-24572231. One of the reports behind this speech was research by Age UK (2013: 29–32) specifically on rural areas.

as, by and large, an extremely friendly place, which they believe to be in stark contrast to the cold and unfriendly character of metropolitan areas. People in The Glades often remark how it is virtually impossible to go walking in the village without being greeted by others, at the very least with a smile and a 'good morning'. Very frequently people stop to chat. Most people assume they will talk with, and not just buy from, the local shopkeepers. As an ethnographer, I spent a considerable amount of time in public spaces such as coffee shops and pubs, and it is easy to see how many people are greeted by name and known to each other. In public spaces, the village corresponds to the ideals of traditional friendliness and warmth. Even more impressive is the level of philanthropy and voluntary service, exemplified here by Celia (8), Gerald (9) and Elizabeth and Richard (13). This is fully confirmed by the sheer level of volunteering at the hospice itself, even if volunteers are generally modest and reticent about making claims for their labour. How then can we reconcile this evidence for undoubted generosity and ubiquitous friendliness of these villages with the isolation of these terminal cancer patients? The two forms of evidence could hardly be more opposed.

To explain this discrepancy, we need to consider the private and the public as two distinct modes of socializing. The interviews showed that the preferred mode always takes place within what people regard as the public domain. They greet and chat in the street or when shopping. They socialize at village events such as the annual carnival, or at a performance of a cultural society. Some people use the sports clubs, others the pub. Two primary catalysts that allow strangers to converse are babies and dogs. People also confirmed, and I observed, a classic trope of English sociality, which is that neighbours really do talk over the garden fence in both front and back gardens.

This friendliness in the public domain is contrasted with a powerful rule that respects the autonomy of what they consider to be private, reflecting traditional sayings such as 'an Englishman's home is his castle'. In particular, working-class informants or those living in the smaller villages avoid going into each other's homes. The one exception is when people are rearing young children – a period of intense inter-domestic sociality since children happily invade the private spaces of other families, bringing parents together. The main time for creating long-lasting friendships has become mother-and-toddler groups. But this is only for a short period, after which there is a consistent fear of being seen as imposing oneself upon the time or interests of others and especially of being viewed as a nosy or inquisitive neighbour. The English assumption is that other people have better things to do than be interested in oneself, with a common fear of being boring or boorish if one imposes. The core characteristic here is social reticence.

This causes problems for the hospice when someone like Emma (10) admits that she keeps refusing the help she actually needs because she doesn't want to be a burden; so nor does Vanessa (16). Elizabeth and Richard (13) only want to discuss what they do for the hospice as volunteers, rather than acknowledge a debt to it. What is striking is that they are hugely involved in public sociality and yet may suddenly admit to bitter feelings of being neglected by the people they felt closest to who, since the diagnosis of cancer, have backed off rather than rallying around. They know all the neighbours, yet after describing various people who don't visit them and talking about elderly people whom they help because no one else is doing the visiting, we find just one positive story about how they are going to receive a visit in their home. Far from being spontaneous, they inform us that this is now arranged to take place in two weeks' time. It's astonishing how formal and awkward a visit for tea in the home appears to be, given that this is one of the most socially involved couples one could ever hope to meet.

Looking at the subsequent loneliness of the elderly, we can see a common trajectory. Several men, for example, used to have many friends at the pub, but when illness meant a decline in mobility or that drinking was no longer possible, the people they drank with do not subsequently come and visit the home, leaving the individual largely to himself. A similar pattern follows with regard to the golf club or the other areas and institutions of public sociability. Informants told me that when they reached retirement they deliberately engaged with new activities such as golf or amateur theatre because of their fear of isolation, but the strategy fails when they can no longer frequent such sites due to illness.

Typically, people are constantly assured that if ever an ailing individual should need anything at all by way of help they should feel free to ask. The phrase 'You only need to ask' was almost a mantra during this fieldwork. These offers seem entirely sincere. The reason that they come to nothing is simply because of the next step that is required. To be proactive in giving any help, without having been specifically asked, is to be intrusive. To be proactive in actually asking for specific help is equally intrusive. As a result, in many cases the isolated individual cannot approach or be approached by those living in the area, such as their neighbours, even when both sides wish this to happen, which is typically the case.

There is no such embarrassment involved when the care is given through formal channels. So these same neighbours feel free to engage in public support through volunteering. Indeed, they may end up giving support, through the hospice, to people they might have cared for, but cannot otherwise support, as members of the same community or neighbourhood. Ideally, however, volunteering should result in caring for strangers since there is less embarrassment involved. Primary carers, such as husbands, wives or siblings, often become just as isolated as the patients for precisely the same reasons.

If this book was set in London, these results might not seem especially surprising. In a previous ethnography of shopping in North London (Miller 1998), I worked in typical urban working-class housing estates. There I found 'salt-of-the-earth' housewives who had lived in adjoining properties for several decades but had never seen the inside of each other's flats, even though they were obsessed with keeping up interior appearances just in case any outsider should ever enter. But this was nothing new. Michael Young and Peter Willmott (1957) carried out the most famous study ever undertaken of a British community, subsequently published as *Family and Kinship in East London*. This population was the heartland of working-class community. Yet here too we find the same pattern – immensely friendly on the outside but an avoidance of visiting the inside (1957: 107–10), a domain largely restricted to kin. With regard to rural areas, Strathern (1981: 125) also found that in a traditional village people expected neither cousins nor neighbours to enter their home, only very close family. It is quite possible that in northern England, neighbourliness may be more sustained, though there are similar concerns with autonomy and nosiness (Edwards 2000: 128–34).

All this prior work suggests that the behaviour described here is in no way specific to the elderly. It is simply the traditional pattern of social life in southern England. An example would be what Fox (2004: 401) terms the English 'social dis-ease', which includes embarrassment, insularity and awkwardness, leading to a sense of discomfort and incompetence in the field of social interaction. My ethnography provides greater specificity by showing how this social embarrassment can actually be more of a problem for intimate relationships than for interactions with strangers. My informants gave many grounds for legitimating this reticence. A common reason relates to the foundational assumptions of reciprocity. If you give to or do something for a person, it imposes an expectation that one will have to reciprocate, leading to a fear of being in their debt. Less predictable seems to be a deep concern with revealing how fundamentally uninteresting people often assumed that they would be to others.

My informants also generally assumed that, in as much as this was a problem today, it must be because of some kind of decline in social life. Everyone believed that the 'traditional' English family and neighbourhood were more intensive and supportive. It is often said that the turning point must have been the 1950s, prior to the eruption of modernity in the sixties and following what has been termed the 'myth of the Blitz' (Calder 1992) as the icon of idealized English social solidarity. But is this true? Fortunately, the 1950s was also the context for one of the few precedents to Fox's *Watching the English*, an anthropologist named Gorer (1955) who wrote a book called *Exploring English Character*. Based on a questionnaire sample of 5,000, he describes a situation that sounds very familiar. Isolation might be greatest in London 'but what is perhaps surprising is that the next loneliest type of community, judging by this criterion, are the small towns and villages' (1955: 51). With respect to neighbours, he notes,

The typical relationship of the English to their neighbours can probably best be described as distant cordiality. Some two-thirds know most of their neighbours well enough to speak to; but not one in 20 know them well enough to drop in on without an invitation; and it is very exceptional for neighbours to entertain one another for a meal or to spend an evening together. Two-thirds of my respondents pay no formal visits to neighbours in this fashion. (1955: 53)

Only 8 per cent felt they could entirely rely on their neighbours (1955: 55). The main response was a litany of complaints about neighbours.

Furthermore, the population in the 1950s had a similar nostalgia. They too believed that there must be some earlier period in which people were much friendlier. This pattern repeats itself as one goes back in time. A recent book by Cockayne (2012) examines the history of neighbours. In the 1880s, a social worker, Nellie Benson, again bemoans the standoffishness of neighbours and sees this as a decline from some previous period (2012: 210). Cockayne notes that even historians of the early eighteenth century observe an unwillingness to burden neighbours with one's own concerns (ibid.: 39). In summary, she suggests that historically neighbours saw far more interaction than today, but this is a history of necessity and mutual dependence based on poverty, not an expression of sentiment. In short, we have no historical evidence that this ideal of domestic sociality was ever an actual contemporary practice, yet it was always present as an expression of nostalgic loss. At every historical period, people believed that in some previous era things had been different and friendlier. The sentiment fuelling Brexit clearly has very deep and historical roots.

Many of the patients confirm a deeper historical context. Vanessa (16) reports the legacy of older concerns for respectability: 'Mum was really into respectability, yes. I had a friend who lived just along the road and his mother was divorced and my mum really frowned on that. She was never really a mixer so we never really got into the habit of doing things like that. I never went to clubs or anything.' Her father, a sergeant, was equally aloof from wider society. Others not included here recall a similar parental concern with respectability. *Social Media in an English Village* documents how new social media such as Facebook represent a threat precisely because of the way they seem to blur the boundaries of the public and the private.

So it seems there are strong academic grounds for seeing this situation as reflecting a deep history of a particular English style of socializing. But this still begs one critical question. If this was merely an issue of friends and neighbours, it would not cause the degree of isolation found amongst these hospice patients. It was always assumed that the primary carers would be the family. Surely families are close by default, even when neighbours and friends are not? The evidence from this book says otherwise. The quotations provided above speak as much to relatives as to friends. Often, there seems to be a sense of a natural attrition, as in the following case:

Grandchildren, as they get older, get in contact less, I think that's often the way. The little eight-year-old from the local primary school, she's in to see me occasionally. Yes, we've got quite a close relationship. And I have with all my grandchildren but they've grown up. The eldest one is now married so I hardly ever see her, you know. John, he's 22 now, he'll occasionally zoom up on his motorbike and come and see me but not a lot. They're so busy working, you know. He's in retail. They're forever at work. Don't think I've seen Linda now for 6–9 months. Next one down I saw a couple of weeks ago. He might come every 2–3 months, then the other one who's now 15, she's gradually dropped off seeing us. She would only come if her mum or dad were bringing her because it's out of the way for her. Don't speak to them on the phone, no, as they get older. Just less close.

Betty and Gloria (6) also show this powerful desire to keep the family at a distance from their true condition and needs. There are exceptions, such as Sarah (1), who uses her terminal condition precisely to try and heal long-lasting breaches in her family. And we see many close and supportive families such as those of Helen (15) or Gerald (9). Nevertheless, the surprise is the number of patients where the reticence of family seems almost identical to that of non-kin. Again, family isolation is true for a minority, but a significant minority.

From an academic perspective, the history of neighbourhood and community may be matched by key debates on the history of English kinship. Contemporary policy reviews assume a decline in family support, for which the main cause is said to be that children live at an increasing distance from their parents (e.g. Age UK 2009). But Gorer (1955: 43) suggests that even in the 1950s children in the south of England were least likely to live with their parents and there was a similar discourse about the break-up of the family, which was assumed to have been more integrated in some nostalgic past.

This leads to one of the most passionate debates about English history, which brought together both historians and anthropologists. In an excellent and comprehensive survey of the history of these debates, Tadmor (2010) notes the continuity in this basic assertion that there must have been some historical decline of the family. But this is challenged both by historians (e.g. Laslett 1977, 1983), demographers and anthropologists, such as Alan Macfarlane, whose book *The Origins of English Individualism* (1978) suggested that, unlike continental Europe, English families seem to have been largely nuclear in orientation even prior to any form of 'modernity'. Furthermore, 'Even relief for the elderly poor, historians emphasized, was provided through parish support, rather than primarily through the support of kin' (Tadmor 2010: 19). Historians of the family assume support must have come from community while historians of community assume it must have come from family. Actually, then as now, it seems the English preferred institutionally provided support. Tadmor also shows that subsequent historians provide a more nuanced and diverse picture with less dualism between nuclear and extended families, or individualism as against kin. One of the clearest critiques of the assumption that the family has declined or that we have lost 'family values' that were once prevalent is found in Gillis (1997: 51) who points out that in some ways this lack of family support probably dates all the way back to medieval times when life itself was so fragile that families were highly transient.

There is, however, one change that probably has exacerbated this distancing from family, a change in what might be called the ideology of 'family' itself.[6] In recent decades, we have seen a global shift in the relationship between friendship and kinship. Generations ago, kinship was the dominant idiom, leading to what anthropologists called 'fictive kinship'. Older readers will

---

[6] I explore this in much more detail in a forthcoming paper called *The Ideology of Friendship in the Age of Facebook*.

remember a time when it was common for close friends of one's parents to be introduced as 'aunty' this or 'uncle' that, although not actually blood kin (e.g. Freed 1963). This was because using kinship terms expressed the closeness of a relationship. Today, we have moved to the opposite situation, where a person may be introduced as 'my mother, but also my best friend'. This reflects what has become the 'the idealness of friendship' (Paine 1999: 41) centred increasingly upon notions of 'autonomy, voluntarism, sentiment and freedom' (Bell and Coleman 1999: 10). There is a general sense that such connotations provide a bulwark against various structures of oppression and obligation which can include the feeling that kinship itself has become a burden (Obeid 2010). In short, friendship has replaced kinship as the dominant idiom because we see the freedom of choice in friendship as more authentic today than the obligations to relatives that stem from birth.

As a result, in the past relatives might have seen their responsibilities to their families as unequivocal and given by the central role of kinship itself. But making family relationships more like friendship relations may have weakened that sense of fixed obligation and made the fulfilment of these roles a little bit more optional, so that now kin can face the same kind of ambiguity over responsibilities of care as friends. Again, this is only a trend. Mostly, families do rally round and give the support one would expect. But there is clearly enough evidence for the neglect of kin obligations to require this more detailed explanation.

To conclude, we need to resist the temptation to follow the patients themselves in their assumption that if people are not always providing the comfort that might have been expected, this must be because of the decline of some traditional form of community or family life. Against this, Victor (2003; see also

Victor, Scambler and Bond 2009) claims that the number of elderly people in England reporting themselves as lonely or isolated has not significantly increased since the major survey of 1948. Indeed, the figures show remarkably little variation over time. It seems that after examining both social science and the historical evidence, we must face the conclusion that the problem we are facing is not the loss of English tradition – the problem is English tradition. This is precisely why we need today, as we have always needed, the support of institutions, such as the hospice, rather than a presumption of family or community support assumed to be some kind of organic or natural source of care.

Recommendations for Hospice Use of New Media

As a final contribution, I have briefly summarized here the practical suggestions that arose from the research (for more details see Miller 2013). The last paragraph already provides one such strong recommendation. I have found that the hospice as an institution is not invading some established world of more 'organic' social and community care and replacing it with institutional care. Without the hospice, in many cases there simply would not be any similar provision. For example, several carers noted that the only time they ever speak to other people about their work as carers is through the monthly carers' meetings organized by the hospice. Far from replacing community, it is the hospice as an institution which creates community.

For these English patients, one of the most difficult consequences of illness is the loss of dignity. In talking about their condition, they prefer the company of other patients who suffer from similar kinds of cancer and who can therefore discuss, with much less embarrassment, their commonly held problems of bodily dysfunctionality, which they know others would find distressing and embarrassing (see also Lawton 2000). It is another reason they prefer professional to informal social care.

The other more general recommendation that comes directly from the evidence within this volume is for an assault on the cult of abstract ethics and confidentiality. An obsessive concern with patient confidentiality and ethics seems to be the single major cause of harm to patients other than disease itself. It creates considerable fear amongst staff and is probably a case of something that is widespread today, an underlying fear of litigation masquerading as ethics.

Versions of several of these recommendations have started to appear since the time this research was completed.

Establish a 'patient digital creativity' website

Health services should stop spending huge sums on bespoke IT systems created by corporations and sold back to health services at considerable cost. Creativity has moved from commerce to the unpredicted appropriations by ordinary users of ubiquitous devices, such as smartphones and apps, which change every few months. Those with special needs and their families will, from now on, be the vanguard in adapting ordinary commercial media to their specific requirements. A memorable example was when an elderly lady had been advised to adopt her recipe-book stand for her iPad so that she could FaceTime without her hands shaking.

We require instead a 'patient digital creativity' website (or Facebook page) where health-care professionals, such as nurses, who visit patients in their own home and see the evidence of this creativity, while retaining patient anonymity, post observations of innovative patient's usage of new media. These can be read by other nurses and clinicians who then inform their own patients with similar issues or problems. Similarly, information can be shared with regard to failures, feedback and other consequences. In short, we need to establish a much more extensive and dynamic set of peer-to-peer networks of information whose foundation is the creativity of their patients and families, and which are constantly kept up-to-date through everyday observations.

The use of digital technology and new media

Hospices should ensure access to good wireless broadband and mobile reception, and if patients do not have their own device, they should be able to access a laptop with a webcam, set within a private room. By now, this should be regarded as an essential facility for all such institutions.

There was, however, another problem uncovered by the research which was that nursing and other staff seemed very unsure about the institutional attitude to their own use of new media, often assuming that this was forbidden. This in turn reflected the obsessive and unwarranted concern with confidentiality. They need to be directly informed of clearly defined policy which states that this is not the case, and that unless told otherwise they should assume that the use of all new media is to be encouraged in order to take full advantage of the ways these connect them to patients and improve patients' welfare. This includes webcam, email, texting, Googling, blogging and smartphone apps where appropriate.

The hospice is complemented by the rise of online forums which provide a wide range of communities, some more anonymous than others. Although there are plenty of patients who have found these for themselves, it would surely do no harm if hospices and other medical institutions took a proactive role in helping ensure that patients were knowledgeable about the possibilities and range of such support forums, while also recognizing that, as shown in this volume, there are also patients who specifically do not want to be identified or categorized by their disease.

Establish a 'digital buddy' scheme

This proposal is to establish a support scheme whereby volunteers working for the Hospice visit people in the home to help set up or maintain such computer facilities as they desire. This might include, for example, downloading information and training in the use of Skype, removing unwanted spam and viruses, showing how to use voice-activated software and helping find specialist software and equipment for those with physical disabilities. The volunteers would visit at the behest of the community clinicians who have identified the need. Without wishing to assume gender stereotypes, and while this would be open equally to males and females, it should be noted that currently the hospice volunteers are overwhelmingly female and this scheme might attract males who have not yet identified a niche within which they feel able to provide hospice support.

Staff noted that typically younger carers and relatives buy IT equipment as something concrete they feel they can 'do' for elderly patients. They want to teach them usage since again it gives them something to do, and even volunteers look for tasks, beyond making tea for patients, that can be fulfilling. So in some cases the potential resource is there but needs more systematic direction and induction into the more appropriate slow, sustained and gradual modes of help that do not overwhelm patients, who may resent enforced IT assistance.

Establish a 'notes to share' scheme

Currently note-taking by nurses varies considerably from handwriting to the use of obtrusive laptops. The research suggested that the ideal was the use of a tablet from which the nurse could access the patient's record database. A tablet is preferred because, as a horizontal device, it does not impose a vertical screen that symbolizes a barrier between nurse and patient but rather appears as an instrument for sharing information. This could then be used alongside patients to jointly look up relevant information, e.g. where can I locally buy a support device?

Polymedia and the practice of patient choice

Our research demonstrated considerable variation in individual patient preferences regarding communications with professional staff and also friends and relatives. This reflects our ideas about polymedia (Madianou and Miller 2012a) and the way that people navigate a diversity of new media channels. We need to be curious about individual choice and cannot assume that we know which medium suits each person in every situation. For example, some individuals prefer to receive painful and/or complicated information via email rather than in a face-to-face consultation because email provides space and time to assimilate and process what is being conveyed. The choice of medium can be an important gesture of power and control. In a relationship where patients are almost always in a submissive, powerless position, anything that gives them some measure of control will help reconcile them to the developing relationship with their carers. Giving them the decision over which medium of communication they prefer to use in different situations provides this additional benefit.

We propose that this question of media preference is given for situations such as news about their prognosis or information as to the regime they are expected to follow, the organization of future meetings and, later on, preferences for family members in bereavement. This becomes a small addition to the initial set-up meetings that routinely take place between staff and patients on first encounter. There is no expectation that any staff should read an email at 2.00 a.m., only that a patient is free to write one at that time – having a reassuring auto-response with emergency alternative telephone numbers may help.

Creation of a patient/carer charter for new media use

Apart from the fear of retribution from health authorities for unlicensed usage, the main concern of staff is that the spread of new media might leave them open to various forms of harassment from patients or carers. They might blur requisite borders between hours of work and non-work and the boundaries between professional and non-professional relationships. The principles at stake here are not, however, unduly complex and generally reflect values and expectations held throughout the community. Much of the most problematic behaviour, such as stalking of nurses by male patients, is already subject to legal prohibitions.

Nevertheless, new media make it so easy to cross boundaries that we may need a new charter to be given to patients and carers of what the hospice regards as appropriate and inappropriate use. One part of this should state clearly that where a patient is deemed by a nurse or other member of staff to have used media inappropriately, then that member of staff has the right to terminate that particular channel of communication. Hospices will vary in the degree to which they feel it necessary to have patients make indirect contact through the hospice rather than directly via the work phones or work emails of staff.

Proactive expansion of patients' social relationships

The single major finding of this research is the degree of isolation and loneliness even in villages. The social universe, especially of older males, can be remarkably small, and social contacts tend to diminish with decreased mobility. Facing severe illness or having just lost a spouse are the worst times to try and introduce new media to facilitate social contacts. This is often a time when people have also lost hope and confidence. But hospices might end up having to provide less staff support, if they were proactive earlier on, in helping patients use social media to retain communication with family and friends. Instead, relevant volunteers or the patients' families might be enlisted rather than encroaching on staff time. While no one should impose media on unwilling patients, hospice staff can predict contractions in social support which the patient has yet to experience.

e-listening/consultation service

Models from the Samaritans and some hospices demonstrate the utility of services directed to young people who prefer to share their feelings via digital media. This sort of service may be part of the hospice website and could be useful for bereavement counselling and also for those with terminal conditions.

Both anonymized and personal versions are possible and serve different needs.

Some further possibilities might include the provision of anonymity for those who wish to express feelings that are generally regarded as illegitimate, or illegal, and where it is possible that being able to express such fears and desires may help prevent their actual occurrence. A patient who cannot express themselves face to face for social reasons, might do so under the cover of an e-Listening service. For example, a nurse was frustrated by her visits because 'he says about two words during every visit, because she [his ever-present wife] says everything. He completely relies on her.' An e-Listening service might also work for carers who are often the ones most in need of sites for self-expression. In addition, if sufficiently resourced, a hospice may consider having an 'ask-the-doctor' provision on their website.

Recommendation of internet information sites

From the point of view of health services, there is a vast range of information that could be invaluable to patients. It seems a real pity that there is no recognized international 'kite-marking' scheme that helps users of the internet to distinguish between established medical information based on research and evidence (backed by governments and medical authorities) and sites that are either entirely ill-informed or most commonly hide a commercial imperative or interest beneath the facade of pure provision of information. The normal process of 'Googling' for health information fails to differentiate between these very different kinds of material. Over the next few years, this problem is going to become acute because we can predict a huge increase in mHealth through smartphone apps.

As a result, medical staff are increasingly having to spend time combating the profusion of 'treatments' that colonize the internet, largely reflecting commercial interests. On the other hand, the same process means that patients may be better informed and discussion can proceed at a much higher level than before. Since it is unlikely that we will see kite-marking any time soon, it seems reasonable for the hospice to provide all patients who use the internet with a list of recommended online sites or, increasingly, phone apps that they feel patients would benefit from (or conversely should avoid). Such a list imposes no restrictions and patients may continue to browse as they see fit, but this acknowledges that the internet is not a neutral space and helps combat the increasing impact of commercial sites posing as medical information.

Digital legacy apps

Some hospices have had discussions with individuals who have been developing specific digital legacy apps which are designed to help patients think about their digital legacy. Increasingly, there will also be digital assets whose disposal requires real consideration, such as email accounts, social media accounts and music collections (see also Walter et al. 2011). It also refers to the use of online facilities to bequeath materials ranging from poetry to birthday wishes. Staff who have used such an app with patients in a consultation have found that it helped them in initiating conversations about intimacy. One patient said, 'I hadn't been able to talk about my funeral until I used the app. It gave me an indirect way of talking to my husband without actually having to voice the "death" word.' In general, advice on how to use ubiquitous sites such as Facebook is more useful than bespoke apps.

Skype/webcam visiting service

Skype or webcam interaction could be delivered by trained volunteers to offer social support to isolated patients or as an effective way for nurses to review stable patients. But, as both patients and staff note, this represents a positive to the degree that the webcam is used to replace the phone call, and a negative to the degree that the webcam is used as a substitute for face-to-face visits.

References

Age UK. 2009. Loneliness and Isolation: Evidence Review, http://www.ageuk.org.uk/documents/en-gb/for-profes sionals/evidence_review_loneliness_and_isolation.pdf?dtrk= true

Age UK. 2013. Later Life in Rural England, http://www.ageuk. org.uk/Documents/EN-GB/Campaigns/Rural%20campaign/ later_life_in_rural_england_report_LR.pdf?dtrk=true

Bell, S. and Coleman, S. 1999. The Anthropology of Friendship: Enduring Themes and Future Possibilities, in S. Bell and S. Coleman (eds), *The Anthropology of Friendship*. Oxford: Berg, pp. 1–20.

Calder, A. 1992. *The Myth of the Blitz*. London: Pimlico.

Cockayne, E. 2012. *Cheek by Jowl: A History of Neighbours*. London: Bodley Head.

Dahlberg, L., Andersson, K. and Lennartsson, C. 2016. Long-Term Predictors of Loneliness in Old Age: Results of a 20-year National Study. *Aging and Mental Health*, pp. 1–7, 1 November 2016, http://tandfonline.com/doi/ abs/10.1080/13607863.2016.1247425?journalCode=camh20

Edwards, Jeanette. 2000. *Born and Bred: Idioms of Kinship and New*

Reproductive Technologies in England. Oxford: Oxford University Press.

Fox, Kate. 2004. *Watching the English: The Hidden Rules of English Behaviour*. London: Hodder and Stoughton.

Freed, S. 1963. Fictive Kinship in a North Indian Village. *Ethnology* 2(1): 86–103.

Gillis, J. 1997. *A World of their Own Making: A History of Myth and Ritual in Family Life*. Oxford: University of Oxford Press.

Gorer, G. 1955. *Exploring English Character*. New York: Criterion Books.

Laslett, P. 1977. *Family Life and Illicit Love in Earlier Generations*. Cambridge: Cambridge University Press.

Laslett, P. 1983. *The World We Have Lost: Further Explored*. London: Routledge.

Lawton, J. 2000. *The Dying Process: Patients' Experiences of Palliative Care*. London: Routledge.

Macfarlane, A. 1978. *The Origins of English Individualism*. Oxford: Wiley.

Madianou, M. and Miller, D. 2012a. Polymedia, Communication and Long-Distance Relationships. *International Journal of Cultural Studies* 15(5): 1–19.

Madianou, M. and Miller, D. 2012b. *Migration and New Media: Transnational Families and Polymedia*. London: Routledge.

McGoldrick, M. and Gerson, R. 1985. *Genograms in Family Assessment*. New York: W. W. Norton.

Miller, D. 1998. *A Theory of Shopping*. Cambridge: Polity.

Miller, D. 2008. *The Comfort of Things*. Cambridge: Polity.

Miller, D. 2013. Hospices: The Potential for New Media, http://www.ucl.ac.uk/anthropology/people/academic-teaching-staff/daniel-miller/mil-28

Miller, D. 2016. *Social Media in an English Village* London: UCL Press.

Miller, D. et al. 2016. *How the World Changed Social Media*. London: UCL Press.

Obeid, M. 2010. Friendship, Kinship and Sociality in a Lebanese Town, in A. Desai and E. Killick (eds), *The Ways of Friendship: Anthropological Perspectives*. Oxford: Berghahn Books, pp. 93–113.

Paine, R. 1999. Friendship: The Hazards of an Ideal Relationship, in S. Bell and S. Coleman (eds), *The Anthropology of Friendship*. Oxford: Berg, pp. 39–58.

Saunders, C. 2006. *Cicely Saunders: Selected Writings 1958–2004*. Oxford: Oxford University Press.

Sherwood C., Kneale, D. and Bloomfield, B. 2014. The Way We Are Now: The State of the UK's Relationships 2014. Relate, https://www.relate.org.uk/policy-campaigns/publications/way-we-are-now-state-uks-relationships-2014

Shriver, L. 2010. *So Much for That*. New York: Harper.

Strathern, M. 1981. *Kinship at the Core: An Anthropology of Elmdon, a Village in North-West Essex in the Nineteen-Sixties*. Cambridge: Cambridge University Press.

Tadmor, N. 2010. Early Modern English Kinship in the Long Run: Reflections on Continuity and Change. *Continuity and Change* 25(1): 15–48.

Victor, C. 2003. *Loneliness, Social Isolation and Living Alone in Later Life*. Economic and Social Research Council, http://www.researchcatalogue.esrc.ac.uk/grants/L480254042/read

Victor, C. and Bowling, A. 2012. A Longitudinal Analysis of Loneliness amongst Older People in Great Britain. *Journal of Psychology* 146(3): 313–31.

Victor, C., Scambler, S. and Bond, J. 2009. *The Social World of Older People: Understanding Loneliness and Social Isolation in Later Life*. Maidenhead: Open University Press.

Walter, T., Hourizi, R., Moncur, W. and Pitsillides, S. 2011. Does the Internet Change How We Die and Mourn? Overview and Analysis. *Omega: Journal of Death & Dying* 64(4): 275–302.

Young, M. and Willmott, P. 1957. *Family and Kinship in East London*. Harmondsworth: Penguin.